P9-CDU-998

The State Universities and Democracy

Allan Nevins

THE STATE

UNIVERSITIES

AND 37904

DEMOCRACY

——

University of Illinois Press

Urbana 1962

(✩)

Introduction

*Ever since the founding of the University of Georgia in 1785
as the first state university, our public institutions of higher
learning have been imbued by a spirit of liberalism and democracy. In a large and healthy sense, they have been political institutions. As they spread westward, grew in numbers, and
throve in vigor, they lent support to the abiding doctrines of
democracy.*

When Condorcet wrote his Sketch of the Progress of the
Human Spirit *in the shadow of the guillotine; when Jefferson
sent Peter Carr his controversial letter of 1814 outlining a full
system of state education; when John Stuart Mill declared in
the wake of the Chartist Movement that British educational
life must respond to this "revolt of nearly all the active talent
of the working classes against . . . the ruling classes"; when
Jonathan Baldwin Turner asserted in 1850 that liberal education "must begin with the higher institutions, or we can never
succeed with the lower"; and when H. G. Wells made his
memorable statement that mankind faces a race between education and catastrophe, they expressed one fundamental belief.
It was the belief that all men have a potential capacity for*

right reasoning if proper agencies, and particularly educational institutions, will free that capacity from corrupting restraints. The American state universities expressed this belief more realistically and energetically than the free universities in London and Manchester, Heidelberg and Freiburg, Brussels and Paris.

When the Civil War began, the United States had twenty-one state colleges and universities, with more at the point of birth. The Land-Grant Act which Lincoln signed in 1862 accelerated a process which, seventy-five years old, had already attained telling results. If Justin S. Morrill's enactment had never gone on the statute books, every state would in time have had its tax-supported university, for the example set by Virginia, Missouri, and Michigan was too sound and fruitful not to be followed. The material resources provided by the Morrill Act were important. The moral encouragement was an equally effective stimulus.

Most important of all, however, was the democratic impact upon higher education, for the law annexed wide neglected areas to the domain of instruction. It kept before our fast-growing population the vital necessity of developing — by research, by the organization of scattered elements of knowledge, and by careful application of scientific principles — a truly expert cultivation of technology and agriculture. In the one field it promoted the emergence of the most effective engineering schools on the globe. In the other it lifted land-use to a wholly new level, and in time established a connection between the national government and the academic world which provided an appartus for research and for the rapid general diffusion of scientific discoveries, unparalleled elsewhere. Widening the gates of opportunity, it made democracy freer, more adaptable, and more kinetic.

American universities have been criticized on many grounds. Thorstein Veblen, objecting to their organization for efficiency, called them "factories of erudition." Bryce, and many others, thought their sense of values distorted; they have produced graduates socially more mature, but intellectually decidedly more immature, than the best European seats. Various critics have deplored their latter-day size, though if a university is skillfully governed it can combine size with intimacy, and Paris with 67,000 students and California with 45,000 can reach the individual about as well as Oslo or Princeton with 3,500. Few, however, have ever criticized the contribution our public universities have made to democracy. Norman Foerster did so a generation ago, emphasizing a contention that they were training the Jacksonian mass instead of centering their efforts upon the Jeffersonian elite — for Jefferson wished to sieve out the "best genius" among each forty pupils for higher education. But for better or worse we have a mass democracy; the universities must reflect it; and they have recently learned a great deal about special tuition for the "best genius."

These lectures, delivered at the University of Illinois to mark the centennial of the Morrill Act, attempt a brief examination of four stages in the development of the state and land-grant institutions, with special attention to their services to democracy. Such a treatment is of necessity impressionistic and incomplete, but I have tried to give it human interest as an introduction to a striking and somewhat neglected phase of our history.

The Huntington Library   ALLAN NEVINS

(☆)

Contents

(I)

THE IDEAS

OF THE FOUNDERS

WHEN THE plan for a system of land-grant colleges took shape, with the result that President Buchanan vetoed a bill for its creation and that President Lincoln signed the measure, it could safely be said that no true university existed in the United States. It could also be said that throughout the Western world a many-sided revolution in theories of higher education was gathering force.

Henry Cabot Lodge tells us that when he entered Harvard in 1867, the winds of the revolution were about to sweep away its ancient mustiness. "I went in," he writes, "under the old system, and came out under the new. I entered the college of the eighteenth century with its 'Gratulatios' and odes and elegies in proper Latin verse . . . the college with the narrow classical curriculum of its English exemplars, and came out a graduate of the modern university." Brander Matthews, who entered Columbia College in 1868, found it a place of almost incredible isolation, stagnancy, and eighteenth-century primitivism. He was treated like an unruly schoolboy; he never walked into the college library of fewer than 15,000 volumes; and until near the end of his school days he never heard a modern idea. Then he, too, perceived a change. He listened to Henry N. Rood deliver a truly useful set of lectures on science. At Yale, Thomas R. Lounsbury finished his four years without once hearing mention of any English author — and Yale did not change.[1]

The Crystal Palace Exhibition in London in 1851, and its immediate reproduction in New York, had been a spectacular demonstration that the world had entered upon a new age. Every year the faith of the Western nations in progress was strengthened by social, scientific, technological, and cultural advances. For Americans in particular, every fresh invention, from sewing machines to telegraphs, every new application of power, from locomotives to liners, every industrial innovation, from oil wells to Bessemer steel, opened stirring vistas. Anything seemed possible to the nineteenth-century civilization that was conquering one land after another by the industrial revolution and a new social enlightenment. Against this background the college education of earlier times seemed hopelessly antiquated; it had to be wrested out of the ruts in which it had so long traveled. A revolt against it grew, compounded primarily of four elements: rejection of the tyranny of classical and theological studies, championship of science, insistence on attention to agriculture and the mechanic arts, and — most important of all — a demand for greater democracy in education.

I

The revolt against the classics had been under way since the days of Wilhelm von Humboldt in Prussia and Jeremy

[1] Henry Cabot Lodge, *Early Memories* (1913), 181 ff.; Brander Matthews, *These Many Years* (1917), 101-112.

Bentham in England. In Germany, even in the eighteenth century, the new universities at Halle and Göttingen had taken on a more practical character than the old, while the technological high schools at Freiburg and Brunswick had gained great prestige. When Prussia lost Halle to Napoleon's new kingdom of Westphalia, the University of Berlin was founded in 1809, incorporating the already famous Prussian academy of science; and Humboldt, who had been made minister of instruction, helped give it principles which raised it to a foremost place in Europe and assisted in the regeneration of all Germany. He, Niebuhr, Neander, Fichte, Hegel, Schelling, the brothers Grimm, and others lent it an unapproached breadth of instruction. Its *Lehrfreiheit* ministered to its astonishing growth in fame and number, for in that bracing atmosphere professional work flourished. All truly literate Americans, especially after the publication of Victor Cousin's famous report on Prussian education, knew of it, and many attended it.

Bentham published his *Papers upon Codification and Public Instruction* in 1817, and the success of the University of Berlin helped encourage his disciple Lord Brougham to lead in creating the University of London. Over this institution Bentham, who was widely read in the United States, still reigns as tutelary spirit. Favored visitors to its University College are shown his skeleton, clothed and seated in his favorite chair, with his skull fronted by a wax mask. Nobody did more than Bentham and his other disciple, James Mill, to emphasize the power of education and its social importance. Copies of Bentham's *Westminster Review* carrying these ideas swam after 1824 into scores of American newspaper offices and hundreds of homes.

Anyone may find an eloquent expression of the English

revolt against the tyranny of Greek, Latin, and moral philosophy in the writings of James Mill's great son, John Stuart Mill. He believed thoroughly in a liberal training, but he had no patience with the kind of Oxford that Gibbon had described, "steeped in port and prejudice," and relying exclusively on the classics. Mill's essay on Guizot not only pays tribute to the great Frenchman whose book on modern history, much used in American colleges before and after the Civil War, was one of the broadening influences of the time, but enters a plea for the systematic study of politics, history, and society. Adam Sedgwick of Cambridge, a famous geologist, published a discourse on the studies of his university; and this inspired Mill to write a scathing essay on what he termed the intellectual "degeneracy" of the country and of the universities therein. The once great seats of learning, he declared, had ceased to furnish the world either sound knowledge or inspiring ideas. Moreover, they were complacent in their retrogression. "All is right so long as no one speaks of taking away their endowments, or encroaching upon their monopoly."[2]

[2] Literate Americans by 1850 were familar with the ideas of the Germans named, and Sybel and Schleiermacher as well, particularly as such men as George Bancroft, John Lothrop Motley, George Ticknor, and Longfellow brought them home from German study. They followed closely the leaders of British thought. Several Frenchmen, however, were almost as well known. Guizot's *History of Civilization in Europe,* founded on his famous lectures at the Sorbonne in the three years from 1828 to 1830, was widely used in American colleges, his work being the more acceptable because he was a Protestant. Of these lectures G. P. Gooch writes: "He left an ineffaceable impression on his hearers. Jules Simon declared that he was eloquence incarnate. . . . He appeared to his audience to treat of human affairs as if he stood above the petty struggles of humanity." Reading of the enthusiastic crowds that Guizot, Cousin, and A. F. Villemain drew as they alternated at the Sorbonne, and of the stir they excited in the minds of aspiring French youth, many Americans asked, "Why can-

Meanwhile, in America such men as James Dwight Dana, Francis Wayland, and in due course John Fiske and E. L. Youmans, took up the battle against a narrow classical discipline. They were abetted on a more popular front by reformers of the type of Horace Greeley. That the struggle was nearly as much needed in the young republic as in Europe is proved by the reminiscences of the men who went to the old-style colleges and by an examination of the standardized and routinized curricula of the ante bellum period.

A round indictment founded on such an examination was offered by James A. Garfield, graduate of Williams, former army commander, and member of Congress, in an address which he delivered at Hiram College in Ohio on June 14, 1867. He had examined the catalogues of some twenty Eastern, Western, and Southern colleges, finding them all alike. To get a bachelor's degree in Harvard College, which was typical, the student on leaving a district school must thereafter devote four-sevenths of his time and labor to Greece and Rome. Even in a course labeled nonclassical the situation was nearly as bad. "In the whole program of study, lectures included," declared Garfield, "no mention whatever is made of physical geography, of anatomy, physiology, or the general history of the United States. A few weeks of the senior year given to Guizot, the history of the Federal Constitution, and a lecture on general history once a week during half of that year, furnish all that a graduate of Harvard is required to know of his own country, and the living nations of the earth. He must apply years of arduous labor to the history, oratory, and poetry of Greece and Rome; but

not *we* have such a center of fresh learning and inspiration?" G. P. Gooch, *History and Historians in the Nineteenth Century* (rev. ed., 1954), 178-184; and John Stuart Mill's essay on Guizot in the *Edinburgh Review* (October, 1845).

he is not required to cull a single flower from the rich fields of our own literature. English literature is not named in the curriculum."

This was the Harvard that Charles W. Eliot was about to reform. And how much the reformation could accomplish is evident from a passage in Eliot's *A Late Harvest*. The law and medical faculties gave their degrees to any man who had paid three term bills covering eighteen months and had not been very irregular in attending lectures. "When I asked in the Medical Faculty in 1870 if it would be possible to substitute an hour's written examination for the five minutes' oral examination (a five minute interview with the professor of each of the nine principal subjects then taught in the school) at the examination for graduation, the answer came promptly from the Head of the Faculty: 'Written examinations are impossible in the Medical School. A majority of the students cannot write well enough.' "

But scores of colleges were precisely like old-time Harvard. "No wonder," said Garfield, "that men are demanding, with an earnestness that will not be repressed, to know how it happens, and why it happens, that, placing in one end of the balance all of the mathematical studies, all the physical sciences in their recent rapid developments, all the principles of political economy and social science which underly the commerce and industry, and shape the legislation, of nations, the history of our own nation, the constitution of government, and its great industrial interests, all the literature and history of modern civilization — placing all this, I say, in one end of the balance, they kick the beam when Greece and Rome are placed in the other." This tyranny of custom, said the future President, must end.

II

The situation was the more intolerable because most intelligent Americans since the days of Benjamin Franklin and Count Rumford had followed the steady rise of science and knew much of its benefits. A championship of scientific studies was the natural second element in the general revolt. Benjamin Thompson, Count Rumford—the American who founded the Royal Institution in London in 1799—had taken as keen an interest as Franklin, Benjamin Rush, and Jefferson in theoretical science. Benjamin Silliman had started his *American Journal of Science and Arts* in 1818. The activities of Cuvier and Linnaeus, Priestley, Faraday and Boyle, Gauss and Oersted were as closely followed in America as in Europe. Then in the 1830's and 1840's had come a remarkable efflorescence of scientific interest.

A sense of the illimitable possibilities of science, and of its treasury of practical values for a democratic society, lent a romantic coloring to much of the literature of the time. Emerson's essay on "Education," invoking Newton and Humboldt as men who gave humanity a majestic sense of power, asserted that science afforded any youth an unmatchable instruction, for it widened his understanding as nothing else could. "Yonder magnificent astronomy he is at last to import, fetching away moon, and planet, solstice, period, comet and binal star, by comprehending their relation and law. Instead of the timid stripling he was, he is to be the stalwart Archimedes, Pythagoras, Columbus, Newton, of the physic, metaphysic and ethics of the design of the world." Poe's strong concern with biology, which he had studied at the University of Virginia, and mathematics and physics, of which he had learned something at West Point, appears in all his work. The adroit mechanism of half his stories comes from the discoveries of science; his "Eureka" is an essay in cosmogony, and he wrote a famous sonnet "To Science." Readers of Thoreau, Melville, and Holmes met scientific lore and theory at every turn, imbibing a romantic sense of their potentialities. Meanwhile, following the example of Jefferson, political leaders — Albert Gallatin, John Quincy Adams — became protagonists of practical scientific endeavors.

Benjamin Silliman, trained at Yale, in Philadelphia, and in Europe, had lectured widely from the 1830's onward upon a variety of scientific subjects. He gave courses all over lower New England, filled during four years the largest auditorium in Boston, stirred New York audiences, and traveled as far south as Charleston and New Orleans and as far west as Cincinnati and St. Louis to reach fascinated listeners. The geologist Sir Charles Lyell, who also traveled and lectured widely, wrote him from New York in 1842: "Now that I have gone from Niagara to Georgia, and have met a great number of your countrymen on the Continent of Europe, and heard the manner in which they ascribe the taste they have for science to your tuition, I may congratulate you, for I have never heard as many of the rising generation in England refer as often to any one individual teacher as having given a direction to their tastes." It is evidence of Silliman's compelling quality that, although in his two-hour discourses he allowed a five-minute pause midway in which those who were fatigued might drop out, almost nobody left his or her seat.

In the 1840's Harvard and Yale established schools of science, at first obscure, neglected, and impoverished; and in that decade the unique Smithsonian Institution, founded on a bequest to the United States by an Englishman "for the increase and diffusion of knowledge among men," began its work. Its first head was Joseph Henry, then so well launched on his scientific career that when the post was offered him he remarked to a friend, "if I go, I shall probably exchange permanent fame for transient reputation." His fame is actually as permanent as that of the founder, James Smithson. The *Scientific American* was founded in 1845. Next year Alexander Agassiz came to the United States on the wings of his international fame to lecture throughout half the country, and then at once took a professorship at Harvard. American students were traveling in increasing numbers to Scotland, London, Paris, and Germany to pursue science; Eben N. Horsford, for example, later a teacher in the Lawrence Scientific School at Harvard, was studying with the great Justus von Liebig in Giessen in 1844-46. One American publishing house, Appleton's, specialized with great success in the issuance of the best scientific books of both the Old and New Worlds.[3]

When the catalogue of Yale announced in 1847: "Professors Silliman and [John P.] Norton have opened a laboratory on the college grounds for the purpose of practical instruction in the applications of science to the arts and agriculture," this statement recognized work that had really been carried on for five years at private expense. Norton had

[3] Dirk Jan Struik, in *Yankee Science in the Making* (1948), emphasizes the precedence of New England in the adoption of scientific studies. When the Revolution ended, he writes, and for most of the generation following, science had few votaries in the section. In the years beginning about 1830, however, came a mass interest in science and technical questions. By the time that Lincoln followed the Morrill Act by approving the bill which organized the National Academy of Sciences (1863), Yankee science "had grown into American science." But New York, with Rensselaer Polytechnic founded in 1824, had a creditable record, too.

been allowed to become professor of agricultural chemistry, the subject so admirably developed by Sir Humphry Davy and Baron von Liebig, on condition that he draw no salary. A young man from upper New York named John Addison Porter, who had worked with Liebig in the later 1840's, came home to assist Horsford at Harvard and then to succeed Norton at Yale. Soon afterward he married the daughter of the wealthy Joseph Sheffield. As a consequence of his success in arousing the interest of his father-in-law in his teaching, the Yale Scientific School in 1860 gained the Sheffield name and fortune and began taking new strides. One early stride was particularly noteworthy: as the Civil War drew on, Porter arranged a short course in agriculture which brought about five hundred farmers into New Haven for scientific lectures.

III

The revolutionary demands in higher education had a broader base, however, than a mere rebellion against the classics and a demand for the installation of science, political economy (as economics was then called), history, and modern literature in its stead. The effulgent midday of science was almost at hand: Herbert Spencer would publish his *Principles of Psychology* in 1855 and Darwin his epochal *Origin of Species* in 1859. With the great Victorian luminaries, Dickens and Thackeray, Tennyson and Browning, Meredith and Trollope, not to speak of bright American stars, filling the literary heavens with light, it was becoming impossible to deny the claim of letters to academic attention. The political and economic revolutions of 1850-70 in the United States called for a curricular recognition of their principles and backgrounds. But meanwhile the so-called "industrial movement" of the era, the transformation of the practical arts, thrust a bold set of claims into the academic sphere.

Higher instruction, said the industrial leaders, must be brought into harmony with the needs of a practical, growing people. President Francis Wayland of Brown University told his trustees in 1850: "Lands were to be surveyed, roads to be constructed, ships to be built and navigated, soils of every kind, and under every variety of climate, were to be cultivated, manufactures were to be established which must soon come into competition with those of more advanced nations; and in a word, all the means which science has provided to aid the progress of civilization must be employed." The classics and humanities should be supplemented by subjects helpful to industrial and agricultural progress; subjects that would lift the farmer and mechanic out of their old limitations. What we want, proclaimed Horace Greeley, are men with the expert skills to double our grain crops and fertilize and beautify all the green hills and valleys.

This concept of industrial schooling involved a pedagogical theory that reached down to first principles. Rousseau had declared: "Education comes to us from nature, from men, and from things." The oldest universities, from the days when students flocked to Salerno, Bologna, Oxford, Paris, and Cambridge to gather at the feet of a few eminent teachers, had acted on the theory that education came from men, their books, and their lectures, quite ignoring nature and things. Harvard, Yale, and Princeton had followed them. The innovators now intended to put nature and things, meaning applied science and the land, into the forefront of the university scheme, thus effecting a revolution in objects and methods. The task, as represented by the tool, the machine, the stockpen, and the farm, would hold equal place in education with the savant.

The skilled teacher, of course, would remain essential. As Aristotle had written, men learn by doing and become good builders by erecting houses, lyre players by practicing on the lyre, and magistrates by making just and sagacious judgments. They must perform these functions as experienced builders, lyre players, and judges do them, and should learn from the most proficient exemplars. But man would no longer be the only essential; the field, workshop, and laboratory, representing nature and things, would be equally vital. Behind these theories the industrial movement in education also put a moral imperative. It was the gospel of the innate dignity of Work, so eloquently expounded in 1843 by Thomas Carlyle in his book *Past and Present*. "All true Work is religion," he wrote, quoting the old monkish dictum, *Laborare est Orare* ("Work is Worship"):

Older than all preached Gospels was this unpreached, inarticulate, but ineradicable forever-enduring Gospel: Work, and therein have well being. . . . What is immethodic, waste, thou shalt make methodic, regulated, arable; obedient and productive to thee. Wheresoever thou findest Disorder, there is thy eternal enemy; attack him swiftly, subdue him; make Order of him, the subject not of Chaos, but of Intelligence, Divinity, and thee! The thistle that grows in thy path, dig it out, that a blade of useful grass, a drop of nourishing milk, may grow there instead. The waste cotton-shrub, gather its waste white down, spin it, weave it; that, in place of idle litter, there may be folded webs. . . .

All true Work is sacred; in all true Work, were it but true hand-labor, there is something of divineness. Labor, wide as the earth, has its summit in Heaven. Sweat of the brow; and up from that to sweat of the brain, sweat of the heart; which includes all Kepler meditations, all Sciences, all spoken Epics, all acted Heroisms, Martyrdoms — up to that "Agony of bloody sweat," which all men have called divine!

It was in answer to this demand for industrial education that John Addison Porter had given his short course of agricultural lectures at the Sheffield Scientific School early in the 1860's. For the same purpose the Sheffield school offered a course of eighteen lectures to mechanics in the winter after Appomattox; a great tax on the overworked professors, says a university historian, but much appreciated by the mechanics, and hence continued year after year. But the old academic sections of Yale still looked with suspicion, if not hostility, upon what they called the "new education."

The first strong public enunciation of the idea of agricultural colleges in America came from Simeon De Witt, surveyor-general of the state of New York, early in the nineteenth century. He knew that Britain, France, Germany, and even Russia had agricultural schools and that the United States had none. De Witt, who by a curious stroke of fate bought most of the site of present-day Ithaca, and made his home on East Hill there, published in 1819 a pamphlet, "Considerations on the Necessity of Establishing an Agricultural College, and Having More of the Children of Wealthy Citizens Educated for the Profession of Farming." What he proposed was a state college, which should include provision for experimental reseach. After this Lieutenant-Governor James Tallmadge of New York made a report in 1826 recommending a School of Agricultural Mechanics and Useful Arts. In this, he predicted, "the manufacturer, the journeyman, apprentice and laborer will become the pupils." The idea grew and was taken up by some of the very active agricultural societies in the various states. John S. Skinner, editor of assorted agricultural and industrial journals, petitioned Congress in 1848 for state subsidies to be used in founding colleges of agriculture and mechanic arts. Though most farmers were skeptical, he found supporters.[4]

At the beginning of the 1850's, Jonathan Baldwin Turner stepped forward with a plan for a state industrial university in Illinois, which he outlined in speeches in the towns of Griggsville and Granville. The response was enthusiastic, though nobody knew just how his dream could be realized. He himself soon discovered the best expedient: federal land grants to the states. He published in the *Prairie Farmer* a letter explaining how the nation's vast public domain lay awaiting constructive use. "And I am satisfied," he confidently asserted, "that if the farmers and their friends will now but exert themselves they can speedily secure for this State, and for each State in the Union, an appropriation of public land adequate to create and endow in the most liberal manner, a general system of popular Industrial education, more glorious in its design and more beneficent in its results than the world has ever seen before." This was in March, 1852; and in the following year the Illinois legislature sent Congress a set of resolutions declaring that a system of industrial universities, liberally endowed in each state, would develop the people and "tend to intellectualize the rising generation."

[4] One reason why agricultural schools arose tardily in the United States was that agriculture in the older states moved only slowly from self-sufficiency, of the type described by S. G. Goodrich ("Peter Parley") of Connecticut in his *Recollections of a Lifetime* (1856), to a specialized status, and moved slowly also in mechanization. When Emerson spoke to a Massachusetts cattle fair in 1858 he took as title "The Man with the Hoe"; his farmer was still a manual worker. But that same year McCormick manufactured nearly 4,100 reapers. The structure of farming was being changed, especially in the Midwest; and with the change came a demand for professional status and training. Cf. Sigfried Giedion, *Mechanization Takes Command* (1948), 130-168.

A legislative request could accomplish little; a member sitting in Congress could do a great deal. Years before Justin S. Morrill secured election to the national House from rural Vermont, he had expressed the opinion that it would be well to slice off from the colleges a portion of the antique European studies and substitute some that were newer and more practical. He was unquestionably acquainted with Turner's ideas, for he heard them discussed in a meeting of his state agricultural society. But by the middle 1850's ideas upon vocational education flowed in from many sources, and Morrill, a thoughtful man of wide reading, possessed a vision, an acumen, and a persistence all his own. Like Turner, he believed in breadth of education — in founding institutions where students might pursue almost any subject. He later told a group of educators that the bill he devised was not intended to create mere agricultural schools; that he opposed class legislation for farmers alone; and that he "wished the teaching of science to be the leading idea."

When Morrill's bill came before Congress in the late 1850's, a few agricultural colleges were weakly struggling into existence. The Michigan legislature in 1855, and the Maryland legislature the next year, established such institutions, while Pennsylvania authorized the opening of a farmers' high school. These were the pioneers. The Michigan college at Lansing stood quite apart from the state university at Ann Arbor, which had made its true start much earlier, in 1841. Wisconsin also already had a state university, which had gotten uncertainly under way in the 1840's, but the state founded no separate agricultural school. In due course agricultural instruction would be incorporated into the university. Thus Michigan and Wisconsin set two examples which, consciously or unconsciously, other states later followed. Iowa created its separate agricultural college like that at Lansing. Illinois founded an industrial university which broadened into a state institution of a comprehensive character comparable to the University of Wisconsin. So did Minnesota, and so did California. Other states varied in policy and practice. That Jefferson and his cofounders of the University of Virginia early in the century would have approved of the Wisconsin plan of a broad unitary institution rather than the Michigan plan of a division of interests, there can be little doubt.

IV

Great social changes are never effected by ideas alone, but they are never effected without them, and without passion behind the ideas. The most important idea in the genesis of the land-grant colleges and state universities was that of democracy, because it had behind it the most passionate feeling.

As strongly as men espoused the revolt against old-style classical education, as warmly as they championed science, as much as some of them were stirred by plans for industrial instruction — none of these causes enlisted their feelings like the cause of greater democracy. A fundamental emotion gave force to the principle that every child should have free opportunity for as complete an education as his tastes and abilities warranted. Jefferson had planned a somewhat restricted application of this principle, and Turner, Greeley, Ezra Cornell, Justin S. Morrill, and their allies carried it into wider territory.

Social and economic democracy in America means primarily liberty of action and equality of opportunity. The central idea behind the land-grant movement was that liberty and equality could not survive unless all men had full opportunity to pursue all occupations at the highest practicable level. No restrictions of class, or fortune, or sex, or geographical position — no restrictions whatsoever — should operate. The struggle for liberty when carried to its logical conclusion is always a struggle for equality, and education is the most potent weapon in this contest. Democracy implies intellectual liberty with full freedom to think, write, and speak. It implies an open society, without caste lines, giving its members full freedom to move from calling to calling, rank to rank; and a mobile society, with equal freedom to move geographically, to change environment, and to find without agonizing effort new positions or fields of enterprise.[5]

It was this ideal of an open, mobile society that Ira Allen had in mind when in the last years of the eighteenth century he pledged six thousand pounds — more, alas, than he had, for he died a pauper — to found the University of Vermont. His real bequest was not money but a dream, a vision. The dream was of an institution to give full education to worthy people even if they were penniless. "It is not the rich man

[5] Carl Becker writes that Andrew D. White, cofounder of Cornell University, adhered to the liberal-democratic creed of his century. He believed in "working for freedom of opinion in order that truth might prevail, for freedom of status and occupation that careers might be open to talent, and for freedom of government in order that no man might be compelled against his will." *Cornell University: Founders and the Founding* (1944), 77, 78. Horace Greeley tells us that he believed that democracy required education to be "free and common as air and sunshine": "To this end, we must have seminaries which not merely provide work for their pupils, but *require* it inflexibly from all — which educate the head and the hand together, each to be the ally and the complement of the other. . . . Only through a true and nobler education can the working masses ever attain the position and respect which the genius of our institutions predicts and requires for them." *Recollections of a Busy Life* (1868), 509, 513.

that I am calculating to assist," he declared in his peculiar English, "as the poor, the rich may send their sons to what college they please but the poor have it not in their power. Yet they may have the most promising posterity and if they can obtain good educations may be in time rulers of the land." In this era of the self-made man every American knew the possibilities of our open society. Everyone had read of the rise of ill-schooled Ben Franklin to the Royal Society; of Washington's career without benefit of college; of Henry Clay's self-tuition when a friendless and moneyless emigrant from Virginia to Kentucky; of the way in which Stephen A. Douglas, coming from Vermont to Winchester, Illinois, at nineteen, with his coat over his arm and fifty-nine cents in his pocket, had made himself master of many subjects. Most people knew how Joseph Henry, whose formal education ended in Albany academy, had given discoveries of the first order to science before he became head of the Smithsonian. It seemed important to throw the gates still wider open.

The names of the early state institutions — the Universities of Virginia, Georgia, North Carolina, Vermont, Wisconsin, Michigan — remind us of a significant fact in the history of higher education. Regionalism, or relevance to a special community, had never affected the pattern of German universities. Many of them were placed in small towns, where they cultivated a detached, unworldly spirit. Students migrated freely from seat to seat, without local or district ties; Tübingen, Heidelberg, Halle, Bonn, Göttingen, had little or nothing to do with the small states in which they found themselves. The University of Berlin was German rather than Prussian. So, too, in Scotland and England the universities were national rather than regional. That could certainly be said of Edinburgh, Glasgow, Oxford, Cambridge, and the University of London, which drew so much of its inspiration from Berlin and Göttingen. It was not until Mason College in 1900 became the University of Birmingham that the idea of regional service penetrated British academic thought. Joseph Chamberlain, Birmingham's most eminent son, had said two years earlier: "To place a university in the middle of a great industrial and manufacturing population is to do something to leaven the whole mass with higher aims and intellectual ambition."

But in the United States the idea that universities should have a regional function took firm root from the beginning. Harvard was planted for the special inspiration and behoof of Massachusetts Bay, and William and Mary for the Old Dominion. The country was so large that as higher education spread westward it had to find a state or regional pattern, just as the nation was so practical minded that the spirit of academic work became in increasing degree utilitarian. America became the home of universities which combined a world outlook with adaptation to special environments.

The note of American life was hopeful, exuberant expansion, and, as for two centuries past, the exuberance was founded upon a sense of the freshness, wealth, and future greatness of the West. Men, women, and children would continue to stream westward by road, canal, river, and railway; the line of settlement would be pushed deeper into Iowa and Minnesota and beyond Kansas and Dakota to the foot of the mountains, fresh furrows turning up rich black soil that had never before glistened under the sun; the crossroads' general store and blacksmith shop would give birth to a village, and the village, to a town. The weekly Springfield *Republican* or New York *Tribune,* the battered copies of Pike's *Arithmetic* and *Peter Parley's Book,* the Bible, and the franked *Congressional Globe* would go westward with the settlers. Here and there a man would rise up to found a weekly newspaper, a school, a church; the first log cabins would melt away like spring snow to be replaced by frame or brick houses. In these houses would swarm children: bright children, to get their ideas out of the hard-shell Baptist preacher, out of some humble counterpart of Mentor Graham, out of the aunt who came visiting from Philadelphia, out of the land-office receiver running for Congress; and to get an aesthetic impulse from a stray copy of the *London Art Journal* that came floating through the community.

Everywhere in the mid-century republic were men who saw that despite flood and drought, Indians and desperadoes, sectional war or no war, growth would gather force; men who realized in 1850 that within thirty years Illinois would have more than three million people, Missouri, more than two million, and Kansas, one million — that this Midwestern area, with opulent cities, a shining reticulation of rails, an ever thicker punctuation of the map by courthouse domes, church spires, and business blocks, would be an empire — with another empire burgeoning on the Pacific from Monterey to Puget Sound. From knowledge of the past they felt certain that this land would teem as no other on the globe with bold, confident, ambitious men. They knew that the population would include a sprinkling of longheaded squires from New England, commodores from New York, and Eastern-bred ministers of learning and spirituality, and Germans and Britons trailing garments, however tattered, of Old World cultivation and manners. They were aware that into these energetic communities a steady fall of seed would come from lyceum organizers, traveling scientists, touring politicians, teacher-training schools, Eastern publishers, and art unions. And all the while the families of bright children would multiply, hungrier than ever for ideas, avid for fresh outlooks on the world, and ambitious for station, with among them — who knew? — perhaps new Emersons and Fultons, talents that properly trained could become incalculably valuable.

This vision of rising Western empires, leaning on ever stronger Eastern commonwealths, was pervaded at the mid-century by an assured conception of democracy. Its cornerstone was Jeffersonian equality, the right of every person to an equitable chance in the world, to his innate human dignity, and his fair station before the law. But it now went far beyond the eighteenth-century conception. It was compounded, as we have said, with a belief in a mobile society, moving freely over wide lands, and pushing forward the industrial revolution, that people might seize every opportunity offered. It mingled, too, throughout the North, with a belief in an open society; every person free to think, speak, write, and learn without restraint; free to rise to the height of his or her capacities, defying efforts at social stratification; free to shift from poverty to wealth, from ignorance to learning, and from subordination to command — a society, in short, free in every sense of the word. Finally, the mid-century concept of democracy included a belief that men learned by doing; that the best instruction came from setting their aims high and accepting tuition from trial and error; and that a bold resolution to make the reach greater than the grasp, and to prefer the risky but timely move over the well-planned but tardy course, befitted the national temperament. Let men move forward dynamically; the next generation would profit by their gains and smooth over their errors.

Out of this temper was born the Morrill Land-Grant Act of 1862. It was remarkable as a profession of faith in the future in the midst of civil war; but it was still more memorable as an embodiment of the whole democratic dream of the time and the conviction that the nation must move fast to avoid a betrayal of its imminent needs. Ever in the minds of the leaders was a vision of the families of bright children, springing up by the million over prairie, plain, and foothill, hungry with a New World appetite for knowledge, wisdom, and inspiration. They could no longer be properly served by the small endowed colleges that besprinkled the land — not by them alone; the Hamiltons and Hirams, the Earlhams and Shurtleffs, the Beloits and Appletons. They needed a new education for a new society, lustier, more practical, more energetic, than any society that had previously appeared on earth. Men should not lose a day in striving to create this new education. Should they stop to draw up careful blueprints? — they had no time. They could plan it as it grew. Would they not make costly mistakes? — certainly, as always; but they would learn while they blundered, and they would meanwhile train a new generation in at least semisatisfactory fashion for the paths it should tread. Let them begin; let them fail here, succeed there, and everywhere press on.

And so in the years of the Wilderness and Appomattox, the stormy years of Andrew Johnson's administration, the shabby, sordid years when Grant sat in the White House, the American democracy, fired by its vision, flung itself into one of the grandest works it had ever undertaken: the creation of scores of universities and colleges, on a broad model new to mankind.

(II)

DON QUIXOTE

AND SANCHO PANZA

In the early history of the state universities we can easily find moments of rich significance. It was a significant moment when on August 1, 1818, the President of the United States, James Monroe, two former Presidents, Thomas Jefferson and James Madison, and a score of other men assembled as state commissioners at Rockfish Gap in the Blue Ridge to discuss the site, buildings, curriculum, and faculty of the proposed University of Virginia. Four years later that university began its course. Hardly less significant was the moment in 1852 when the newly chosen Henry Philip Tappan, the first man of piercing vision since Jefferson to shape the destinies of a university, rose in Ann Arbor to proclaim the possibility of rearing there an institution of the best European standards which should be integrated with the whole educational fabric of Michigan. Massive in frame, massive in acquirements and personality, Tappan had placed the University of Michigan in the van of democratic education in science and the liberal studies before a prejudiced board of regents dismissed him after a decade of arduous toil.[1]

And, of course, an immortal moment came when in 1862 Justin Smith Morrill, sitting anxiously in the national House, heard the clerk announce that his College Land bill, already approved by the Senate, had passed by a vote of 90 to 25.

The country will not forget these moments. Nor will it forget the moment in 1864 when another statesman of higher education, Andrew D. White, walking down the steps of the Albany capitol with Ezra Cornell, sketched to him the general design of the university they would soon rear in Ithaca; nor the moment on March 11, 1868, when John Milton Gregory formally received the keys of what is now the University of Illinois; nor the moment in 1872 when Daniel Coit Gilman rose in Berkeley to deliver the wisest and most eloquent inaugural address made by any educator in these years — an address shrewd in its vision of the future greatness of the University of California. Yet significant as these occasions were, they all marked moments of anticipation. They looked to the future; they saw work begin on blueprints of a bridge that the builders were confident would stretch to a far shore, but how, or when, or

[1] The circumstances in which Tappan left the University of Michigan are set forth in Andrew Ten Brook, *American State Universities . . . [and] the Rise and Development of the University of Michigan* (1875), Chap. XII. As two members of the board of visitors wrote John M. Gregory, then state superintendent of public instruction and later head of the Illinois Industrial University, in 1863, the regents had interfered with the interior management of the University of Michigan, had been courageously resisted by Tappan, and failing to overmaster him, had dismissed him. "And a more deadly stab," the visitors added, "was never given to the cause of education, learning, high-toned refinement, and Christian culture . . . throughout the West."

where was uncertain.[2] The full test of the principle of public higher education on a state basis did not come until the Morrill Act was translated into dozens of institutions.

The truly critical hour in the record of every state university, every land-grant institution, struck when the grim hard work of converting blueprints into beams and girders began; when presidents and professors stood at their desks wondering what students if any would come, what qualifications if any they would bring, and what response if any they would kindle at home. Behind the educators lay their dreams; ahead stretched the task of transforming the raw materials of democracy, as yet chiefly bucolic, into what Dr. Gregory termed "clearheaded, broadbreasted . . . men of fully developed minds." This hour for facing reality varied from state to state. Some universities, like that of Wisconsin, were fairly planted before the Morrill Act passed; some, like Minnesota, were half-planted; and some were not to be born until after Justin Morrill died near the end of the century. For most land-grant institutions, how-

---

[2] Gilman's address of November 7, 1872, published with the title of *The Building of the University*, is so wise and eloquent that it should be better known. He offered a broad definition of a university: "a group of agencies organized to advance the arts and sciences of every sort, and train young men as scholars for all the intellectual callings of life." The University of California must not be imitative of older institutions; it must not fail to integrate itself with the state. "It must be adapted to the people, to their public and private schools, to their peculiar geographical position, to the requirements of their new society, and their undeveloped resources." Its principal builders would be the faculty. Gilman emphasized his belief that while the state should provide all essentials, men of wealth should give "the richer and more complete endowment" necessary to high distinction. The first needs of the state were well-organized schools of science and technology, holding the rank long denied them; but this was only half of the proper university pattern. "Let language, history and literature, oratory and poetry and art, still form a chief part of liberal culture. . . ."

ever, the critical hour fell between Appomattox and the centennial year of 1876. This, under the statutory prescriptions for acceptance and use of the gift of national land, was the decade which decided whether enthusiasm and earnestness could conquer multitudinous difficulties; a decade of hard yet eager years.[3]

Spiritually, it stands in our history as a bad decade, stained with Reconstruction hatreds, corruption, and all the errors of the Grant era. Economically, it carried the country through an uneven boom into panic and depression. Yet as a background for the emergence of the land-grant colleges it has its brighter tints. It was a decade of adventurous beginnings, increased social maturity, and rising national self-confidence. The first railroad trunk systems, the first transcontinental line, the first industries organized on a national scale, the first important pools, heralded the day when America would outstrip its European rivals in economic power. Magazines, newspapers, the lyceum, and book publishing all manifested an enhanced vigor. Literature shook off its exclusive loyalty to the Eastern seaboard and

[3] Iowa was the first state to accept the conditions of the Morrill Act, pledging itself to maintain the funds derived from its land grant and to teach agriculture, mechanic arts, and military tactics, without exclusion of literary and scientific studies. Three states agreed to the legislation by the end of 1862; eighteen more before the end of 1865; and sixteen others before the end of 1870. Of the institutions benefited by the Morrill land grants, seventeen had been founded (often feebly) before 1862 — private colleges like Rutgers, state universities like Georgia, Missouri, and Wisconsin, and state agricultural colleges like the nascent schools of Michigan and Iowa. A still greater variety of institutions founded after 1862 soon benefited, the gamut running from Cornell (part state, part private) and Purdue (emphasis on mechanic arts) to Alcorn and Lincoln (Negro colleges in Mississippi and Missouri). Edward Danforth Eddy, Jr., entitles his chapter on the period 1863-79, in his able book *Colleges for Our Land and Time: The Land-Grant Idea in American Education* (1956), "The Struggle."

embraced the West and South. Reform, long chained to the antislavery cause, invaded widening fields, so that men belatedly awakened to the social problem, the labor issue, and the dangers of monopoly. Fresh ideas and aspirations burst into eccentric bloom in Grangerism, the Liberal Republican movement, and the Greenback-Labor crusade. West of the Alleghenies, in particular, the atmosphere gave bracing life to experimental crusades in government, economic arrangements, and education.

We have ample evidence that the academic pioneers who now marched out to tame the wilderness shivered a little; and had they divined the ordeals ahead they would have trembled, for shock after shock awaited them. Almost everywhere the test revealed the same harsh truths. It disclosed the fact that finances were even more icily straitened than they had anticipated; that the academic equipment for satisfying public demands in the fields of agricultural and mechanical instruction was embarrassingly meager; that public support was capriciously uncertain; that both the external hostilities and the internal opportunities for discontent, quarreling, backbiting, and treachery were unexpectedly numerous. While awakening to this grim realization, most of the founders of the new institutions faced severe hardships in ugly environments, with barnlike college buildings, primitive homes, and a chilly social atmosphere. Their pinched stipends meant daily sacrifice. What honor the persevering men among them deserve!

I

The financial rigors they met sprang from dependence on the Morrill Act gift of lands, and the men who managed or mismanaged it; and this subject deserves both a fuller and more discriminating treatment than it has received. At first glance the federal donation to the states of 30,000 acres for each senator and representative seemed a princely endowment. In comparison with the nation's original gift of two mere townships to each new state for a university, a gift authorized in 1787 and thereafter taken as obligatory, it was indeed large. Seventeen states down to the Civil War had benefited from the two townships; several, like Michigan, in an impressive way. But the educators who now pinned high expectations to the Morrill Act bounty realized too late, in general, that it would prove substantial only if well husbanded. Their disappointment was inevitable, but it came hard.

Why inevitable? For one reason, most states found the problem of laying hands on their patrimony highly perplexing. Eight of those in the West still contained enough public land to cover their grants. They could "locate" it at home, sell it, or hold it for higher prices. But other states, like New York, comprehended no public land whatsoever, and still others, like Illinois, contained but an inadequate remnant. The gift to some had therefore to be indirect. The Interior Department issued to each a quantity of land scrip for its allotted acreage. They were to dispose of this scrip to assignees — for of course no state government could take and hold a large area within another state; and they were to keep the proceeds forever inviolate for their land-grant colleges. In this arrangement the government acted as both benefactor and real estate promoter.

A great deal of obscurity yet surrounds the precise disposition made by some states of their share of the Morrill grant. We know that the nation gave away a total of 17,430,000 acres, this being the only endowment the government could then give. We know that the aggregate return from this land slightly exceeded $7,500,000, and that it was not the government's fault that the sum was not larger. Many university historians tend to pass over the disposition of the grants hastily. This is partly because the complexity of statutory authorizations, land locations, sales at various times and places, and modes of investing the proceeds is a dull subject. It is also partly because the story has occasional elements of folly and rascality that make it embarrassing. A number of states let the land scrip slip through their fingers; fingers loosed by negligent officers, pried apart by speculators, or even greased by corruptionists.[4]

It is a matter of rather gruesome interest to ascertain which states did worst in betraying their children. This bleak distinction seems to lie among Rhode Island, Connecticut, Pennsylvania, and New Jersey. When Rhode Island received scrip for 120,000 acres, the legislature assigned it to Brown University for a department of agriculture and mechanic arts. Brown thereupon asked the president and a professional money-raiser named the Rev. Horace T. Love to select the lands. They spent the battle summer of 1863 in the West examining and choosing part of them. Then they returned to report that the task was impossibly heavy, for it involved choosing lands, paying taxes, negotiating sales, and defending titles; and a committee of five headed by the president was appointed to take charge. This body promptly threw up the sponge by selling the whole 120,000 acres to Mr. Love at the end of January,

[4] Typical of much of the haziness in dealing with land grants in Kemp P. Battle's treatment of North Carolina's share in his *History of the University of North Carolina*, II (1907-12), 381 ff.; the reader makes out that North Carolina ultimately extracted about $7,500 a year from its land scrip, but that is all.

1865, for $50,000, taking his notes payable without interest during the next five years. We are not astonished to learn that the sale aroused much criticism. It would be interesting to know more about Mr. Love, who thus obtained so princely a domain at a little more than forty cents an acre.[5]

New Jersey and New Hampshire were hot competitors in much the same folly. When New Jersey was given scrip for 210,000 acres, Princeton and Rutgers squabbled lustily for the prize until in 1864 Rutgers bore it away. And what a prize! State commissioners sold the scrip on a saturated market for a little more than fifty cents an acre, or $116,000, a sum upon which New Jersey obligated herself to pay only 5 per cent a year, or $5,800. The historian of Rutgers shows himself a master of understatement when he writes that this maintained the Morrill idea "in a very modest way." New Hampshire received scrip for 150,000 acres, which the state sold at an average of fifty-three cents an acre, or enough at 6 per cent to yield $4,800 a year. Dartmouth College longed to lay hands on this pitiful endowment, but the farmers in the legislature interposed. Instead, they incorporated a new college to be placed alongside Dartmouth, with an interlocking faculty and board of trustees, its students to have the use of Dartmouth facilities. The creation of this Siamese twin was the only possible means of establishing an agricultural and mechanical college on $4,800 a year.

Connecticut, meanwhile, sold its land scrip for a sufficient sum to provide a little less than $7,000 a year, or enough to add three professors to the Sheffield Scientific School at

---

[5] Walter C. Bronson, *The History of Brown University, 1764-1914* (1914), 333, 334. Mr. Love could echo the Rev. Chadband of *Bleak House:* "Come, let us be joyful!"

$2,300 a year each. A little later, when reinvestment of the funds cut down the income, the salaries were reduced to $2,000 each. And Pennsylvania, which enjoyed one of the greatest opportunities of all, let all her golden chances slip away. The state obtained scrip for 780,000 acres, the second largest grant in the nation. It was assigned to the Agricultural College of Pennsylvania, then a struggling, primitive, isolated school. A few farsighted friends wished to locate the land and conserve it for the future. Against their protests, however, the legislature just after the war decreed the sale of the scrip. Heavy pressure had come from an unholy partnership of land speculators, anxious to obtain a bargain, and officers of the state college, anxious to get funds for a new start. "Together," writes the historian of Pennsylvania education, "they brought to bear an influence which proved irresistible." The speculators obtained nearly all of this immense domain for $439,000, or an average of less than sixty cents an acre.[6]

In the Midwest we meet a somewhat better record. Yet the University of Wisconsin had a rival for Mr. Love in a gentleman who combined the offices of member of the board of regents, speaker of the Assembly, and agent for Caleb Cushing, the famous Massachusetts politician and land buyer. At the beginning of 1866 the university held 240,000 acres, selected and reserved in seven Wisconsin counties, much of it being valuable white pine timberland. Speaker Henry Barron introduced a resolution directing the house judiciary committee to report a bill placing the lands on the market at not less than $1.25 an acre; and the legis-

[6] [Members of the faculty], *History of the University of New Hampshire, 1866-1941* (1941), 34, 35; Frank W. Blackmar, *The History of Federal and State Aid to Higher Education in the United States* (U.S. Bureau of Education, Circular no. 1, 1890).

lation passed at once, ostensibly to give poor settlers farms at reasonable rates, but actually to find its principal beneficiaries in lumber companies, settlement-promotion companies, and wealthy investors. The largest single tract went to Caleb Cushing, for whom Speaker Barron bought some 33,000 acres in Polk County. By 1872 two-thirds of the University of Wisconsin lands had been sold, and by 1885 practically all. The funds derived, $302,000, represented an average price of approximately $1.25 an acre. It was a sacrifice against which Governor Lucius Fairchild and various regents had earnestly but vainly protested.[7]

Illinois countenanced irregularites of a different order. The new Industrial University, as it was called, received scrip for 480,000 acres at a time when, with buildings to erect and equip and Dr. Gregory's contractual salary of $4,000 a year to be paid, it had not a dollar in cash. The trustees therefore instructed the treasurer, in May, 1867, to sell scrip for 180,000 acres at the best possible price. He not only did this but kept on selling. By the end of 1874, according to the report of the state bureau of education, scrip for all but 24,000 acres — that is, for 456,000 acres, one of the largest Morrill Act blocks — had been marketed at an average price of seventy cents an acre. Under the act the receipts, $319,500, had, as we noted, to be invested in an untouchable fund, interest only being available for expenses. Unfortunately, the word "untouchable" was not in the Illinois vocabulary.

The Industrial University direly needed ready money for its start, and knew none could be had from the state. It happened that Champaign County, in persuading the leg-

[7] Merle Curti and Vernon Carstensen, *The University of Wisconsin . . . 1848-1925*, I (1949), 211, 299-301, 302.

islature to give it the new institution, had offered among other donations $100,000 in county bonds. The university trustees now sold this county endowment to the state officers in charge of the receipts from scrip. That is, the university lost the Champaign County gift in a transaction that evaded federal law to make nearly a third of the land-scrip proceeds available for immediate use. The effect of this maneuver was to reduce the Morrill Act endowment from a supposedly well-protected sum of $319,500 to a real sum of $219,500.[8]

Even New York, whose ultimate record appears so conspicuously farsighted, had a narrow escape from disaster. When the state received scrip in 1863 for 980,000 acres, the comptroller took steps to advertise it for eighty-five cents an acre, and 76,000 acres were actually sold at or near that price. Had it all gone at this level, whatever land-grant institution the Empire State reared would have possessed an endowment of only about $800,000. Fortunately the sales soon ceased, for the market had become glutted with land scrip. It was then that Ezra Cornell interposed his wise generosity. This remarkable son of Yankee parents in western New York, tall and angular in frame, slow and austere in manner, grimly concise in speech, cloaked under his rough exterior a boundless benevolence. Chin-whiskered, sharp-eyed, large-nosed, he comes as close as anyone in our history to looking like the popular image of Uncle Sam, and

[8] Burt E. Powell, *Semi-Centennial History of the University of Illinois,* I (1918), 279-280. The university could not be said to have lost money, but it had lost the state guarantee for a substantial part of its land-grant revenues. Had Lincoln's state, the richest in the West, been less stingy it would have furnished ready funds for a beginning. C. P. Slater, *History of the Land Grant Endowment Fund of the University of Illinois* (1940).

it might be well if Uncle Sam had all his best traits. He at once saw what could and should be done. He would pay the university about $300,000 in cash for the unsold scrip, 813,920 acres; he would engage ultimately to double this sum as the land-grant endowment; and he would hold the lands for an advance, paying all profits into the university exchequer as his own endowment.

The transaction, stated in these somewhat oversimplified terms, appears today one that should have been easily completed and certainly profitable. It did not so appear when Cornell proposed it in 1865, nor was it actually consummated without difficulty and anxiety. But its ultimate consequences completely vindicated Ezra Cornell's noble foresight. Partly because of the time interval which his money and credit offered, and partly because of the acumen with which the scrip for more than a half-million acres was located in potentially valuable areas of Wisconsin pine, Cornell University by 1905 had received from its land grant $5,765,000, or $5.82 an acre. Thus New York, which had been given one-tenth of the Morrill Act bounty, was able finally to pocket more than one-third of all the money it yielded. Among all the new land-grant institutions Cornell University, blest with Andrew D. White's wisdom in formulating its educational policies, began with the sturdiest vigor, and swiftly attained the highest prestige.

Only nine states obtained more than $1.25 an acre for their Morrill land grants, and California alone shared New York's good fortune in getting more than five dollars an acre. Minnesota realized the third-best price, an average of $4.39. The sums received by all the states averaged $1.65 an acre. Illinois in the 1880's obtained $155,000 for 9,000 acres which it had happily kept in Nebraska; that is, it sold these 9,000 acres for approximately half as much as it had earlier obtained for 471,000 acres. What if it had held all?[9] Yet our picture of the fate of Mr. Morrill's great provision must not be painted in excessively dark hues. Several historical considerations restrain us from a rash condemnation of men or measures. One is that the cost of ready money at this time ran at least to 7 per cent; to hold for one year a thousand acres of the average value just noted therefore cost $115, without allowance for taxes; and as interest was compounded, the costs might soon outrun any increment in land values. Another consideration was that Congress, by passing in 1862 the Homestead Act which gave actual settlers a quarter-section free and by simultaneously voting large grants to the Union Pacific and Central Pacific, depressed the value of land. Other railroads soon received wide tracts, which they were naturally anxious to populate. In these circumstances, waiting was not easy. While the West wanted settlement and pressed for a rapid disposal of land scrip, most of the new colleges desperately needed cash in hand for buildings and salaries. After the panic of 1873 business was half prostrate, and even earlier an agricultural depression began which endured until near the end of the century. The wonder was that some states fared as well as they did. Caleb Cushing lost money on the Morrill Act lands that he bought.

Perhaps the most unfortunate fact was simply that the

[9] It was sad that the country had only one Ezra Cornell. When that public-spirited gentleman wrote several wealthy men asking them to help him bear his financial burden, by an investment, not a gift, they all replied praising his generosity, but buttoning their purses. Philip Dorf, *The Builder; a Biography of Ezra Cornell* (1952), 328, 329. Illinois, as I note in my volume on that university (*Illinois,* [1917]) had a citizen who proposed a syndicate for holding part of the institution's lands for better prices; he was abused as a speculator, and got nowhere.

Morrill grant diffused a popular delusion that the new institutions were well provided for, and needed nothing more. Thomas J. Burrill, who taught during these years in what is now the University of Illinois, correctly describes the situation in the decade 1868-78:

> The times were hard, and business was dull. There was little or no successful enterprise afloat. The university was for the industries conspicuously, but the industries were themselves stagnant. Farmers were making precious little headway. The general price of farming land did not advance in Illinois at all during the thirteen years of Dr. Gregory's administration; rather the other way. In the year 1870, some 280 acres of the Griggs farm near the corporate limits of Urbana were sold for $60 an acre, and an offer of $500 was refused for another 40 acres. In December, 1878, eight years later, a committee reported to the Board that an effort had been made to sell another 160 acres of this farm at $40 an acre, and that it had failed. . . . Farm products brought small prices, corn running as low as 32 cents a bushel in 1878. . . . The average acre production in Illinois for the decade 1870-79 was 30.3 bushels. This yielded just about the cost of raising the crop, leaving little for stimulus of any kind. . . .
>
> One governor in the early years told Dr. Gregory, when he was trying to present the needs and claims of the University as a State institution, that nothing could or would be done, adding for emphasis, "The State washes its hands of the whole d——d thing." The records practically support the utterance. Most members of the legislature seemed to think that the university was so richly endowed from the Federal land grant that it was unpardonable presumption to ask for anything more. . . . Other state universities had about the same experience.[10]

Poverty stricken indeed were most of the new institutions at their inception. Evan Pugh, chief founder of the Agricultural College of Pennsylvania, had suggested that a land-

[10] MS Burrill Recollections, University of Illinois Archives. The Homestead Act made no less than 234,000,000 acres available for private ownership without charge. Most investors in the later 1860's and 1870's believed that too much Michigan and Minnesota pine land had been thrown upon the market. Ralph Hidy, Frank E. Hill, and Allan Nevins, *The Weyerhaeuser Company* (1962).

grant college might begin work with a yearly budget of $47,000, most of which would be paid to sixteen professors at $1,500 apiece. Not a single institution except Cornell was within hailing distance of that sum when it began applying the Morrill bounty. Though the University of Wisconsin had been in active operation since 1851, it reached such low water during the Civil War that bankruptcy stared the regents in the face, salaries of the little knot of professors were cut back to $900 a year, and in the fall of 1865 the authorities consoled themselves for a deficit of $1,800 by the fact that they had on hand nearly enough wood for fires that winter. The half-dead University of Minnesota in 1867 was under the ministrations of what its historian calls a pulmotor. Of still others, the less said the better. These were the years of what Earle D. Ross calls "the traditional one-building, crudely equipped, president-professor college."[11]

But the institutions did throw open their doors with a courage half-desperate, half-blind, and wholly sublime. Their reliance on Providence staggers the observer. The secretary of the board of trustees of what is now Ohio State University recorded the belief of that body that a legislative appropriation of $50,000 would place the institution "in such a position of efficiency and usefulness that there will be no need for a long time to come, if ever, to apply for more State aid. . . ." If ever! After all, the ravens had fed Elijah.

II

While scrimping together funds and making pennies serve for dollars, the heads of the newborn institutions faced

[11] James Gray, *The University of Minnesota, 1851-1951* (1951). Mr. Gray elsewhere calls the institution a "grandiose fragment." See Earle D. Ross, *Democracy's College: The Land-Grant Movement in the Formative Stage* (1942), for a thorough record of these years.

the still more urgent problem of enlisting students. Obviously, if they came in a torrent they would bankrupt the feeble colleges, but nobody feared that. It was only at Cornell that they arrived in numbers. The real question was whether they would come in even a trickle. Presidents nervously fingering their notes the first day could recall that when the University of Michigan began in 1841, just six lads had entered.

European onlookers would doubtless have said that universities without a strong supporting structure of secondary schools were castles built in air; but such an utterance would have shown that they little knew how Americans did things. Secondary schools! Since it had required a severe struggle in most states to drag parents beyond the point where they maintained, "All I want my boys to know is the Bible and figgers," and to create even primary schools with sure tax support, secondary schools arose tardily. The Illinois local-option school-tax law of 1825 was promptly nullified by another law providing that no man might be taxed for common schools without his written consent. Ohio did not levy its first state-wide school tax until 1838. Indiana, where Edward Eggleston's Hoosier schoolmaster encountered such depths of rural ignorance and squalor, was still bickering over the issue in 1848-49, the voters dividing so closely in the referenda of those years that the legislature dared not act.

It was while traveling in Indiana just twenty years before the Morrill Act that the agricultural expert Solon Robinson received an Eastern inquiry whether good common school teachers were in demand, and at what price. He replied: "Now if the word 'good' governs teachers, I can't tell. The article is seldom found in this market. If the word 'common' governs teachers, they are tolerably plenty, and common enough in all conscience. The price, $10 to $20 a month."[12] With primary schools few and poor in the West and South, with learning beyond the three R's regarded as superfluous, high schools limped slowly into acceptance. The East had its academies, but the trans-Allegheny region had almost nothing. In the year of Lincoln's election the United States possessed only 243 high schools outside Massachusetts, or about sixteen for each million people. Illinois had ten, Indiana nine, Wisconsin seven, Iowa three, and Minnesota and Missouri one apiece. And how many well-equipped youths emerged from even ten high schools? The Pestalozzian revolution, which substituted true discipline in thought for drilling by rote, obtained no firm foothold in the United States until after 1860. High schools as good as the Thetford Academy which Justin S. Morrill briefly attended were rare, and the atmosphere of most frontier or semifrontier communities fostered not merely ignorance but also pride in ignorance.[13]

One of the difficulties of the new land-grant institutions, indeed, was the pride of the self-taught man in disdain of the Pierian spring. Even Ezra Cornell, when accused of trying to establish an aristocratic university, defended himself in a statement tinctured with anti-intellectualism. "I have no relative," he proclaimed, "of any degree within my knowledge, who is or has been a lawyer, physician, minister

[12] Herbert A. Kellar, ed., *Solon Robinson, Pioneer and Agriculturist: Selected Writings,* I (1936), 351. "Dollars and cents," wrote Robinson of the Midwest generally, "are of so much more importance to many men, than the education of their children, that they are unwilling to incur any extra expense." *Ibid.,* 148-149. This was in 1840, but the statement was just as true in 1860 or 1870.

[13] E. P. Cubberley, *Public Education in the United States* (1934), 198.

of the gospel, merchant, politician, officeholder, gentleman loafer, or common idler — none who have been drunkards or recipients of charity."

In the same spirit Peter Cartwright demolished an Illinois woman who asked him why the prairies had so few doctors of divinity. He rejoined: "Because our divinity is not sick, ma'am, and doesn't need doctoring." Cartwright, who once put down a college-bred Presbyterian quoting Greek by throwing out a sentence of Southern Illinois German, scorned the airs of the learned. "These erudite preachers," he remarked, "remind me of lettuce growing under a peach tree, or of a gosling that has got the straddles by wading in the dew." "My graduation degrees," he boasted, "were taken in and from life's thunderstorms."[14] No wonder that the first announcement issued by the Illinois Industrial University promised that it would turn its back on "mere book-learning."

The most graphic picture of the difficulties faced by the academic pioneers is that drawn in Baynard R. Hall's record of his early days at Indiana Seminary, which grew into the University of Indiana, a picture dating back to the Jacksonian era, but with elements still valid in 1862. Hall, a graduate of Union College, who at first believed that Western colleges might soon equal the best in the East, was brought up short when, as he called the entrants to order on the first day, one rustic answered his question whether they had bought the proper textbooks by an explosion: "Books! I have never heern tell of any books! Won't these ones do, Master? This here's the Western Spellin' one — and this one's the Western Kalkelatur." Another lad announced that he had come to acquire enough bookkeepin' and surveyin'

---

[14] Helen Hardie Grant, *Peter Cartwright, Pioneer* (1931), 125-130.

to tend a store and run a line. Outside, people were demo-
cratically insisting that larnin' — even the most powerful
larnin' — should be bestowed on everybody, and that professors should serve for the honor, or at least be content with
a dollar a day, which was more or double what a feller got
for maulin' rails. Small politicians, according to Hall, were
vociferating: "It is a right smart chance better to have no
collidge nohow, if all folks hain't equal right to learn what
they most liked best."[15]

One land-grant institution, as we have said, astonished
the country by its registration. Cornell opened in 1868 with
the largest entering class to that date in the history of
America — 412 students. Surveying the raw treeless campus
and half-built halls, Ezra Cornell had said at the opening
ceremonies: "We did not expect to have a single thing
finished. . . . It is the commencement we now have in
hand." The record-breaking class had come anyway. They
came because Ezra had beaten all the tom-toms, sending the
general announcement to a thousand newspapers and hundreds of leading Americans; because excited discussion by
friends and foes had greeted the so-called Cornell idea that
in Ithaca anybody could get instruction in any subject; and
because Ezra, to the anguish of President Andrew D. White,
had published in the New York *Tribune* an article promising that students might work their way through by giving
half time to manual labor for the university. A high proportion of the registrants stuck.[16]

The tale in most places, however, was melancholy. At the
University of California the initial registrant, Clarence J.

[15] Baynard R. Hall, *The New Purchase,* James A. Woodburn, ed.,
Indiana Centennial Edition (1916), 322 ff.
[16] Becker, *Cornell University,* 131, 132.

Wetmore, heard Professor Joseph Le Conte say, as he tendered the lad a pen: "It is a distinct honor to be the first student to enter this institution, destined to be one of the greatest in the country." Brave words! But Wetmore had only twenty-six classmates, three of whom dropped out the first year — and at that, California was one of the better-attended universities. At Minnesota a bare handful of students heard the determined William Watts Folwell deliver his inaugural address on September 15, 1869, urging the state to "take the million for her unit" in appropriating university funds. These were words brave to the point of recklessness. The first graduating class numbered just two young men, to whom the people of Minneapolis tendered a banquet. "Two lion cubs!" said Folwell, in a reference to Aesop's fable. The University of Wisconsin had graduated its first class in 1854, again with just two men — whether lion cubs we are not told. The debt-ridden University of Missouri had forty-six students in the year it took advantage of the Morrill Act endowment.[17]

Of these early land-grant students a few had been trained in high schools or academies, and a few by friendly lawyers or ministers. Still others were home taught. Among these last, in Wisconsin, was a youth who came to Madison because he heard that students could board themselves on oatmeal in Scottish fashion for a dollar a week. Sometimes he had only half a dollar. But he proved a true lion cub, for his name was John Muir.

Kansas University held its opening exercises in 1866 with a faculty of three in a gaunt building on a Lawrence hilltop, overlooking prairies still roved by Indians. As the war-

[17] Jones Viles, *The University of Missouri, a Centennial History* (1939), 130.

scarred state had hardly a true secondary school, the brave trio did not expect much. Still, they were startled when they found that the young fellows gathered in the chapel did not include a single youth prepared for standard college work. Scoffers for a time termed the university the "Lawrence High School," and one unfriendly member of the legislature offered to have his wife do all the teaching for $500 a year. At the newly opened University of Arkansas in 1872 sixteen students reported, few if any ready for higher education. "There was nothing to start from," said President A. W. Bishop, "but a farmhouse and 160 acres of land . . . the soil alone to build upon."[18] The Illinois Industrial University began with an enrollment of about fifty, nearly all from Champaign County and its neighbors, and nearly all half-schooled. The West was repeating the history of colonial New England, of which Oliver Wendell Holmes wrote:

> And who was in the catalogue, when college was begun?
> Two nephews of the president, and the professor's son.

The historian of Iowa State College, Earle D. Ross, writes that "democracy's college awaited democracy's high school." On the contrary, its great glory is that it did not wait; where necessary it made itself temporarily into a high school, and as fast as it could it helped create and guide a system of high schools.

For as service to democracy was a necessity, the land-grant colleges *had* to find or make students. One university head said crisply that if the young people could not reach up to the university, the university must reach down to the young people. President John Bascom of the University of Wisconsin coined an equally pungent epigram: "If you

[18] Harrison Hale, *University of Arkansas, 1871-1948* (1948), 16.

make a tree higher by raising its roots above the ground, the tree will die." The new institutions could adopt two courses, not mutually exclusive: they could lower their tests of admission or establish their own preparatory departments, becoming a hybrid of high school and college. In a few instances they temporarily became a high school alone. The first alternative was emphasized by Illinois, and has been described by its second head, Selim H. Peabody: "To secure members the standards of admission were fixed at what were known to be low grades of scholarship. The examinations were mild, and the topics those on which preparations could be made in the common school districts of the state. The students so admitted were employed in their first collegiate years upon very elementary branches of learning. The attendance rapidly increased, but was to a considerable degree ephemeral, composed of persons who came for a term, or for a year, rather than with the purpose of pursuing an extended, consecutive, and symmetrical course of collegiate work."[19]

Peabody added that while this early policy was wise and necessary, its protracted continuance would have prevented the emergence of a true university. Its necessity is clearer than its wisdom, but then compliance with necessity *is* wisdom. This was a fact which those college heads who enunciated loftier and braver ideals soon discovered. Francis Hun-

[19] Nevins, *Illinois*, 58 ff. Youths were urged to "come without fear" to the Illinois Industrial University, where a place would be found for them. The registration from 1872 to 1880 averaged about 350 a year. Peabody, as head, loaned money freely from his own slender means to enable needy students to remain in the university. Katherine Peabody Girling, *Selim Hobart Peabody* (1923), 148. He still encountered much rural hostility, for honest farmers would demand of him, in effect, "What does the university mean to us farming folk but increased taxation?"

tington Snow of Kansas University, for example, declared in 1868: "We aim to be *thorough*, even if we don't graduate a student for ten years. You wonder that so few were ready for the college course, but you must remember that our standard is as high as that at Harvard." With all respect to Dr. Snow, an eminent entomologist and a brave head of the struggling seat on the Kaw, the university did not make good his words even before Populist attacks impaired its efficiency. Folwell of Minnesota also emphasized the cardinal necessity of high standards. Praising the first sons of his university, he told the people: "Had we pursued a different policy heretofore, we could have shown you a greater number today." Yet Folwell, too, had to temper his policy to the tender-skinned lambs who came to his doors. Minnesota gave the lowering of standards a euphemistic phrase: "reaching nearer to the source of talent."

The concomitant establishment of preparatory schools was a policy which had first been conspicuously devised by the University of Michigan. When Tappan became president in 1852 the so-called university was actually only a puny classical academy in Ann Arbor, and while building it into a true institution of higher learning, he reorganized the academy courses into a secondary school. The University of Wisconsin from early days divided its student body into four parts: those in a preparatory department, those pursuing special work without expectation of a degree, those taking normal or pedagogical courses, and those carrying regular university instruction. The preparatory and special groups far outnumbered the regular students. In the year of Appomattox, for example, 290 of the 331 students at Madison were in preparatory, special, or normal work. The same story is told by other institutions. At the University of Arkansas 201 of the 230 students in 1872 were at the high school level, or below it. Poor young men! — the state, scourged by the war, racked by Reconstruction, and in large areas still a frontier land, actually had no other secondary school worthy of the name. It was in a log house in rural Arkansas that, just as the university opened, a boy was born who was destined to be majority leader of the Senate for many years, Joseph T. Robinson; and it was with almost no formal education that Robinson entered the university for two years of study.

Chancellor James H. Canfield used to declare that the University of Nebraska was the thirteenth, fourteenth, fifteenth, and sixteenth grades of the common schools of the state. Some land-grant institutions and state universities for a time did best with grades nine to twelve![20] Fortunately, it soon became clear that the new institutions could effectively encourage the rise of high schools by giving those of sound quality a recognized standing.

The University of Michigan appears to have been the first, in 1872, to institute a system of clear faculty inspection and accreditation. The results were so satisfactory that the universities of Indiana and Wisconsin immediately followed its example, though without the careful safeguards prescribed in Ann Arbor. Minnesota, Nebraska, Missouri, Illinois, and others soon adopted the same system. It was manifestly a sound principle that the state university should be chief guardian of the work of the lower schools upon which it depended. President Folwell of Minnesota had earlier formulated what he termed the Minnesota idea, which required the county and city superintendents to co-

[20] University of Nebraska, *Semi-Centennial Anniversary Book, The University of Nebraska, 1869-1919* (1919), 123 ff.

operate with the regents in creating "a complete, continuous, and effective system of schools," the university serving as regulator and head. But this idea, alas, never took life.

Let us salute the sagacity of Morrill and his cofounders of our land-grant chain of colleges and universities. Actually, to found these institutions before the establishment of effective high school systems was not to put the cart before the horse; it was not to rear a castle in the air without supports. Sound arguments could be adduced for creating the universities forthwith. They called the high schools into being. Suppose the secondary schools, on the prairies and plains, had been established in large numbers first. Whither should their graduates go? To Eastern universities? — they were too distant, too costly, too alien. To denominational colleges near home? — they were little better than high schools themselves. No, they would have gone in nearly all instances from high school into their life work, a prospect hardly exhilarating to ambitious young men or their parents. A community which thought it not worth the financial sacrifice, the struggle, the anxiety, to build, equip, and staff a high school standing alone, would esteem it well worthwhile to create a high school opening into a university. If the horse stood harnessed, anybody could see the value of bringing up a cart. Accreditation stimulated a spirit of community pride. The state universities implied strong high schools, while the high schools did not imply a state university.

III

The search of the new institutions for adequate faculties was in some ways the sternest task of all. Andrew D. White, looking back in 1893, wrote that Cornell had encountered the most dismaying obstacles in finding men of power and repute. The best scholars in 1870 regarded even Cornell as a dubious experiment, blanched at their first sight of the raw campus and the rusticities of Ithaca, and sniffed at the proffered salaries. "I feel surprised," reflected White, "that I was able to secure and hold such admirable men as I induced to come into the college faculty." He set his standards high; better, he used to say, a splendid faculty in a barn than an insufficient faculty in a palace. It was assuredly remarkable that he gained even momentarily the services of Alexander Agassiz, George William Curtis, and James Russell Lowell, and even temporarily such a figure of international renown as Goldwin Smith; that at an early date he secured such scholars as Hiram Corson and Moses Coit Tyler. When White at the very beginning sailed to Europe for equipment and talent, Ezra Cornell saw him off in New York. As the ship left the dock, Cornell, in a sudden afterthought, frantically shouted across the water, "Don't forget the horse doctor!" — and another of White's prizes was James Law, of Edinburgh University, who became the leading pioneer of American veterinary science. But even at Cornell University some departments long remained weak.[21]

Radical leaders of agriculture had hoped to see a wholly new breed of professors, untainted by classical training, stalk upon the land-grant campuses, and were sorely disappointed when they had to enlist men of the traditional disciplines. These men had to accept overwork, meager pay, social contempt, carping criticisms, and unreasonable de-

[21] Not even such distinguished historians of Cornell University as Carl Becker and Morris Bishop can match, in their accounts of its early years, the energy, spiritual fire, and polish to be found in Andrew D. White's two-volume *Autobiography* (1907), of which the Cornell University Press keeps a condensed version in print.

mands. All institutions, old and new, were then familiar
with professors like C. M. Nairne of Columbia, who held
not a chair but a settee. The heroic head of what is now
Louisiana State University, David F. Boyd, took pride in his
ability to teach the entire curriculum,[22] and we frequently
meet such curious combinations as that of a gentleman at
Florida State College who was professor of agriculture,
horticulture, and Greek. Practically all presidents gave part
time to teaching, and much time to extramural lecturing;
nearly all, like Dr. Gregory, toiled without stenographers,
decent clerical help, or modern office equipment, writing
their letters and speeches by hand. Some institutions provided no tenure. In the University of Arkansas, for example,
professors for the coming year were elected just after each
spring commencement, so that all winter no man knew
whether he would hold his place the next fall.

Far off indeed were the days when some land-grant
institutions could outbid the oldest endowed universities for
teachers of distinction. Unthinkable in the West in this period was such a scene as presently took place at Harvard.
"I understand," said Charles W. Eliot, "that it might be
possible to obtain the services of Lawrence Lowell to teach
government. What ought we to offer him?" To which his
chief adviser replied: "Mr. President, offer whatever is
necessary to secure him."[23] That happy kind of scene was
to come, first at Michigan and California, and then in other

[22] Walter L. Fleming, *Louisiana State University, 1860-1896* (1936),
346 ff.
[23] Albert Bushnell Hart in *The Development of Harvard University,
1869-1929*, S. E. Morison, ed. (1930), 182. This volume informs us
that beginning in 1869 the salaries of assistant professors at Harvard
were raised to $2,000, and of professors to $4,000, while tutors stayed
at $1,000. *Ibid.*, p. xli. For decades they remained at this approximate
level.

great state universities, but not for many a year. It was a heavy struggle that Wisconsin had to bring professors' salaries up from $1,200 a year to $2,000; and even the latter sum, as a regent admitted in 1885, furnished little beyond bare subsistence — nothing for travel, nothing for books, nothing for emergencies.

Yet the numbers and quality of the faculties slowly rose. By the centennial winter of 1876, according to the federal commissioner of education, Cornell had forty teachers, California thirty-one, Wisconsin nineteen, Minnesota fifteen, and Nebraska and Kentucky nine each. Such men as Joseph Le Conte and Eugene W. Hilgard of California, William F. Allen of Wisconsin (the fertile-minded teacher of Frederick Jackson Turner and a contributor to almost every number of the *Nation* for a quarter-century), Henry S. Frieze of Michigan, Seaman A. Knapp of Iowa State, and Thomas J. Burrill of Illinois would have ornamented any university in the land. Everyone knew President McCosh's question about any proposed addition to the Princeton faculty: "But mon, is he *alive?*" These men were alive. The wonder is that the early staffs were so strong and that they contained so few misfits such as the University of California found in hiring a journalistic adventurer named William Swinton, innocent of any college degree and with a disreputable record as war correspondent, to teach English literature. Swinton proved a wretched troublemaker.[24] But what good luck and sagacity to pluck a T. J. Burrill out of the Urbana school system!

The history, atmosphere, and leadership of a college or

[24] W. W. Ferrier, *Origin and Development of the University of California* (1930), treats Swinton's activities thoroughly. The man was brilliant but irresponsible.

university were the potent elements in determining the early character of its faculty. Andrew D. White's leadership was daring and imaginative, and he created atmosphere by his lectureships for Lowell, Agassiz, and Curtis. The University of Wisconsin had a history of idealistic effort running back to 1849; it had a friendly, hopeful social environment in the state; and in Paul A. Chadbourne, who became president in 1869, it found a head determined to renovate the faculty. These components created in a few years one of the best teaching groups in the country. And before many years the regents brought to Wisconsin John Bascom, of whom it was said that "he could put twenty Chadbournes in his breeches pocket and walk off and not know it";[25] a scholar and teacher whose inspiration kindled young Robert M. La Follette.

In contrast, the future University of Illinois had no history prior to 1868, no atmosphere, an undependable board of trustees, a pestiferous body of small-minded agricultural critics, and a clam-cold legislature. Missouri was in a still worse situation. The University of Arkansas, when it got started after 1871, was like other Southern institutions in having to seek its teachers in odd nooks and corners. One early faculty member, according to a mordant Arkansas historian, possessed a distinguishing accomplishment over which we hardly know whether to laugh or sigh: "Mr. Brysacher, in his always spotless attire, with a Prince Albert coat, silk hat, and goldheaded cane, was the ideal figure of a cultured, elegant gentleman of the old school. He was very precise and deliberate in his personal habits, and made a punctilious ceremony of partaking of a chaw of tobacco, to which habit he was hopelessly addicted. His spitting, it

[25] J. F. A. Pyre, *Wisconsin* (1920), 192.

was said, was the quintessence of grace and accuracy. With geometrical precision, he could hit the exact center of each cuspidor as he strode up and down the classroom reading his lecture."

Yet, all in all, the early faculties were a heroic breed of men. They struggled valiantly with swollen teaching loads, internal frictions, public distrust, and penury, or an estate near it. We must honor them for their uncomplaining endurance, their persistence, their elevation of mind, and their consecration to the great purposes of state education. Their toil converted a noble but uncertain dream into reality. While a few of them achieved some public recognition, the great majority labored unknown and unapplauded — and contented. In looking back at this age of the great barbecue, of multiplying millionaires, of Godkin's chromo civilization, of so much that was greedy, shoddy, and false, it is refreshing to dwell upon these little groups of self-sacrificing servants of the public good.

IV

The gusts of popular censure and opposition which the land-grant colleges had to face came from various sources. Some of the most vehement attacks were organized by denominational interests, and though they were too ill tempered, selfish, and shortsighted to carry weight, for a short period they threatened to harm some young institutions. New York was not hurt. Andrew D. White, in his delightful account of the church war against Cornell, when pulpit cushions were beaten all over the East against the godless institution, makes it clear that the church did his university more good than harm. They advertised it and sent students to its doors. Johns Hopkins University similarly profited.

Its inauguration included no prayer. Young men, chuckling over the accusation that the trustees had asked Huxley to the opening ceremonies but forgot to ask God, bought tickets to Baltimore. Apparently Western institutions suffered little from ecclesiastical hostility, though the University of Michigan for a time took the precaution of appointing one minister from each major denomination to a professorship. But in the South some real damage was wrought.

In Georgia, for example, Bishop Warren A. Candler, president of Emory College, addressed the legislature in an effort to prove that higher education was no function of a state. It should be left to the churches, which were so magnificently meeting the duty! Other clergymen joined the assault. The head of the University of Georgia reported that pulpits all over the commonwealth had enlisted. "Our scholarship is disparaged; infidelity and irreligion are charged against us. Most exaggerated accounts are given of extravagant living, and parents are made to believe that immorality and vice reign rampant here." That these militant clergymen seriously impeded the growth of Georgia's appropriations for her university, there can be no doubt.[26]

The principal attacks, however, arose from a welter of controversy over the basic aims of the new institutions; above all from agricultural groups who felt that they were being betrayed. In Berkeley, Madison, Ames, Urbana, and

[26] R. P. Brooks, *The University of Georgia Under Sixteen Administrations, 1785-1955* (1956), 85. Selim H. Peabody, a scientist who was sufficiently religious to insist on nondenominational chapel attendance at the Illinois Industrial University, found clergymen eager in the 1880's to assail the institution for teaching Darwinism. He loaned them the chapel for meetings, and one parson was heard to say, as he left the platform: "I tell you, I have given this godless university a good shaking today." Girling, *S. H. Peabody*, 156. It does not appear that such shakings did any harm.

Lexington, a line of battle was drawn between advocates of the traditional literary and scientific education and champions of the new agricultural and mechanical instruction. When university heads declared that industrial education demanded chiefly a mastery of science — biology, geology, chemistry, mathematics — and that for the time being no other teaching could be organized, they incensed men who believed that the manual arts of farm, mill, and workshop could be taught with scientific precision and elaboration. The dispute drew the weak institutions into state politics, for agricultural and mechanical organizations rushed to the capitals to denounce the waste of public money on Latin, modern languages, geology, and calculus.

And the quarrel touched bedrock principles. Men of the practical school felt not merely that their callings were being ignored; they felt still more keenly that their ideal of a democratic education for the hornyhanded as well as the gently bred was being violated. In Britain, France, and Germany all higher education had a taint of caste distinction. English universities, with the porter's lodge guarding the secluded halls, gardens, and tutors' rooms of the colleges, were schools for men who expected training in select professions. An atmosphere of class privilege was perceptible also in the French *lycée* and the German *Gymnasium*. In England the squire's son and merchant's heir might enter Oxford or Cambridge, but sons of the tenant farmer and the blacksmith were shut out. In Germany the peasant only as a rare exception clambered into the *Gymnasium* or university, and the shopkeeper's or laborer's son still more seldom. So it was in France. The cost of nine or ten years' tuition was usually prohibitive, while the social rule that a son should follow in his father's steps was equally a bar.

In America, however, the son of the poorest farmer, storekeeper, and laborer, men felt, ought to have the doors of the people's university flung open to him; not to abandon his hereditary calling, but to find it dignified and lifted to the same plane as the professions. When the land-grant institutions failed to furnish full courses in agriculture they insulted the noble vocation of husbandry, making it seem mean and intellectually impoverished. They struck a blow in the face of the lifelong teachings of Jonathan B. Turner and Evan Pugh. They denied Horace Greeley's assertion that "true Agriculture is a grand, ennobling science, based on other sciences, and its pursuit a liberal, elevating profession"; they questioned Lincoln's emphasis, in his address to the Wisconsin State Agricultural Society in 1859, upon the importance of combining labor and learning — upon the exhaustless profit a trained mind could find in agriculture, where "every blade of grass is a study."[27]

Campus after campus witnessed the same heated drama. University heads laid out and equipped a farm; they hired a professor of agriculture, with assistants; they offered a few tentative courses. With what result? — frustration, anger, despair. President Chadbourne of Wisconsin lamented in 1869: "I do not know of a single Agricultural College that is not encountering violent opposition in its own state; some have gone to pieces, and those most promising are publicly pronounced failures by prominent men."[28]

Hosea Biglow's caution, "You've a darned long row to hoe," was never more applicable. Wisconsin's experience was typically grueling. Establishing a school of agriculture

[27] Greeley, *Recollections*, 296; Roy P. Basler, *The Collected Works of Abraham Lincoln*, III (1953), 480.
[28] Curti and Carstensen, *Wisconsin*, I, 463-464.

in 1868, the university hewed out a three-year course which was simply a segment of the scientific school: botany, zoology, chemistry, geology, and little more. The single agricultural professor was not overburdened. Not one student came to hear him. Not until 1878 did Wisconsin graduate the first two-year student in agriculture, and he long remained the only graduate. A new professor who arrived in 1880 reported that he found no building, no room, no collections, no correspondence, and worst of all, no appropriation.

Elsewhere the story was the same. At Minnesota, after long torpor, the agricultural department by 1877 was giving three puerile courses on "How Crops Grow," "How Crops Feed," and "Farm Drainage." A few students turned up, and stayed or left in an atmosphere of disappointment. Finally Professor E. D. Porter hoisted the white flag. In 1886 he abolished all classroom instruction and degrees, and organized instead a practical school in which young men might do field work at five to fifteen cents an hour. Some students who were kept in a barn rose in revolt. Thereupon Grange leaders threatened to sever the agricultural department from the university, and it took all of President Northrup's diplomacy to avert this calamity.[29] When the trustees of Michigan State College sought an instructor in agriculture, they confessed that they knew not where to find one. Missouri obtained a teacher whose special interest was grapes, hardly an important Missouri crop. The university historian acidly remarks that he failed to communicate to farmers his enthusiasm for the cultivation of artichokes as

[29] Gray, *Minnesota*, 56 ff., 94 ff. A Minnesota professor who toiled for six years to woo the agricultural classes, Gray tells us, once sent out five hundred postcards all but offering rewards for the capture and delivery alive of students, but got only a few direct answers.

a remedy for hog cholera. Some of his utterances suggest an erratic outlook. Thus he thought it worthwhile to say in his course announcement that the farmer did not need work in ethics or philosophy: "He communes with nature so much that his moral powers are better developed. Few crimes are perpetrated by farmers." For a time in the 1870's agricultural courses and students practically disappeared at Missouri.

Meanwhile, the inability of the Illinois Industrial University to organize a school of agriculture precipitated an especially memorable storm. The Chicago *Tribune,* Chicago *Evening Post, Prairie Farmer,* and Jonathan B. Turner himself joined M. L. Dunlap, farmer, trustee, and writer, in denouncing the "parcel of decayed or otherwise incapacitated preachers" who were mismanaging the institution. Early in 1869 the Illinois legislature passed condemnatory resolutions. To the credit of the head, Dr. Gregory, he valiantly stood his ground.

Indeed, the lion-hearted Gregory told critics to their faces that the instruction they demanded was impossible. Opening the first annual short-course of practical lectures in January, 1869, he declared: "Looking at the crude and disjointed facts which agricultural writers give us, we come to the conclusion that we have no *science of agriculture.* Botany is a science — chemistry is a science — but agriculture is not a science in any sense. . . . It is simply a mass of empiricism." This harsh truth made the expert farmers present, including M. L. Dunlap, swallow hard. The short course gave them a series of empiricisms on various subjects from soil to swine, the best lecture being T. J. Burrill's on "Agricultural Botany." Dunlap himself furnished one notable empiricism. Irritated by a statement that New Jersey corn was more nutritious than Illinois corn, he burst out: "It is a fact that when we come to look upon the corn of central Illinois we find a corn that will make perfect whiskey, and is a food for everybody."[30]

But nobody presented systematic instruction. Gregory had hit the nail on the head: a science of agriculture did not yet exist. The brilliant, conscientious, and troublesome M. L. Dunlap was simply a quarter-century ahead of his time.

It was in the University of California that the assailants of literary and scientific education did the most harm. The newborn institution at Berkeley employed a pretentious donkey named Ezra Carr to teach agriculture. A fellow professor has described his approach. "Instruction in agriculture," we are told, "began briskly with a thorough course on fruit-growing in the Garden of Eden, passing rapidly to grain-growing in Egypt, and the conditions surrounding the corner in sorghum which Joseph arranged for Rameses II. . . . It was rapidly approaching Cincinnatus when . . . both instructor and pupils fell asleep while pursuing dry-farming by the encyclopedestrian method of teaching."[31] Limited as Carr was in the classroom, he and William Swinton helped rally the state grange to assail the whole tendency of the university. As in other states, many California farmers and mechanics were outraged to find their sons registering to learn physics, mathematics, English literature, and French. At all costs, they decided, they must

[30] Powell, *Illinois*, I, 304 ff.; and for the proceedings of the short course at Urbana, see *Second Annual Report of the Board of Trustees* (1869), 122-128.

[31] E. J. Wickson, *Eugene Woldemar Hilgard: In Memoriam* (1916).

snatch the industrial departments from their ruinous association with the traditional type of instruction.

For a time they seemed about to succeed. It was only after a savage battle that the university's defenders succeeded in 1874 in obtaining a vote of approval from the legislature and ousting Carr and Swinton. And meanwhile Daniel Coit Gilman, heartsick over the uproar, resigned from California to become head of Johns Hopkins University. "For university fighting I have had no training," he wrote the regents; "in university work I delight." This was a body blow under which the university reeled. He left behind an epigram for men to reflect upon: "Science, though you have built no shrine for her worship, is the mother of California."[32]

One observer wrote in the mid-1870's that not a single land-grant institution had escaped an ugly quarrel over agricultural instruction. On the technological side, by contrast, early teachers were for only a short time forced into shop work, and while some mechanics' periodicals at first attacked every deviation into science as into the humanities, it was not for long. Fortunately for engineering, it was developing with such tremendous vigor that here discontent and quarreling were avoided. As late as 1870, as R. H. Chittenden says in his history of the Sheffield Scientific School, engineering was still a single stem with only budding indications of branching growth. The buds, however, quickly

[32] Fabian Franklin, *The Life of Daniel Coit Gilman* (1910), 143-181. Gilman, who had won a fairly complete victory over all critics and opponents, might have remained at the University of California had he not felt that the institution was too completely at the mercy of legislative caprice. Five wealthy Californians, each of whom had contemplated large donations, told him "that they could not bestow their gifts upon an institution which might be swept away in an hour."

grew into sturdy branches. From civil engineering and mechanics sprang mechanical engineering, electrical engineering, chemical engineering, and other growths. Nowhere was the progress more rapid than in the state universities and land-grant colleges, which indeed became a determining influence in the national development of technology. The fast-growing nation, hungry for many forms of talent, was hungriest of all for engineers. Since the demand for men to open the mines, lift the bridges, drive forward the railroads, and plan the steel plants was so voracious, students crowded into the courses, and teachers developed efficient modes of instruction.

It is difficult to avoid impatience with the more extreme champions of practical education or with the men who forced various land-grant institutions to use the manual labor system, sending students to work in the grounds or fields at a few cents an hour, with the waspish assailants of literature and the classics and with the ignorant commoners who argued that this great new educational undertaking should be held to the level of a set of trade schools or vocational academies. Had they been given their way, they would have ruined the best hopes of the great new adventure. Nevertheless, we must do justice even to these misled folk. If we peer into the background we can muster some sympathy for the frustration and disillusionment of the farmers in particular.

Why was there no science of agriculture by 1870? Three and a half centuries had elapsed since Sir Anthony Fitzherbert, "a farmer of forty years standing," had published his *Book of Husbandry* (1523), the first English treatise on farming. A century and a quarter had elapsed since Jethro Tull did his profoundly influential experimenting and writing in Berkshire upon proper methods of cultivation. Arthur Young's scientific examination into soil fertility was nearly a century old; R. W. Dickson's *Practical Agriculture,* a book soon translated into German and French, had been issued the year of Trafalgar.[33] American farmers knew that George Washington had corresponded with Sir John Sinclair on agricultural principles. They knew that the South Carolina Agricultural Society and Philadelphia Society for the Improvement of Agriculture had been founded in 1784, and that such bodies had since spread to every state.

Studious American farmers were aware, too, that epochal nineteenth-century additions had been made to the shelf of genuinely valuable books on agriculture and horticulture. Sir Humphrey Davy's lectures before the board of agriculture in Great Britain in 1802-12 had opened a new era in the management of soils. His volume on *Elements of Agricultural Chemistry,* a half-century old when Lincoln signed the Morrill Act, exerted a profound international influence. To Americans the name of Justus von Liebig was still greater. His studies in soil chemistry, undertaken at the request of the British Association for the Advancement of Science, had resulted in his *Familiar Letters on Chemistry,* widely read in cheap editions and all the principal languages. It had lifted the theory and practice of agriculture in Europe and America. Liebig was still busy experimenting

[33] John Spencer, farmer and fruit grower of western New York, declared that agriculturists of the Civil War era were prejudiced against books on their calling because they made no advance on the classic works of Tull, Sinclair, and Young: "Nearly all were cribbed from English publications." Philip Dorf, *Liberty Hyde Bailey: An Informal Biography* (1956), 74, 75. A revolt against barren agricultural literature accompanied the other agrarian revolts of the time; but from the time of Buel and Solon Robinson the situation steadily improved.

and teaching when the Morrill Act passed and most of the new institutions opened.

What a stimulus he might have applied had he been brought from his Giessen laboratory in 1870 to make a tour of the agricultural colleges! He had shown just what parts of their nourishment crops derive from humus, from minerals, and from air; he had demonstrated the law of the minimum, that the absence of one essential constituent can make soil barren; he had shown precisely how fertilizers supplied deficient elements; and he had explained scientifically the value of crop rotation — all this in language so polished and elegant that his genius delighted readers while it instructed them.

In sober fact Dr. Gregory's dictum that agriculture was not a science was open to one exception: Davy and Lawes in England, Boussingault in France, and above all Liebig in Germany had made agricultural chemistry a true science. Another subject, farm management, had been taking teachable shape in the hands of Arthur Young in England, Albrecht Thaer in Germany, Jesse Buel in America, and their successors. A great deal was known about animal husbandry. It was men who united organizing capacity, scientific training, and farm experience who were needed — men who could create scientific agriculture — and the impatience of the farmer organizations had some warrant.

Such leaders soon began to appear. They were very different men from the self-taught Isaac Roberts, who presided over agricultural work first at Iowa State College and then at Cornell. Roberts, who boasted that he had no book-learning, but was "a graduate of Brush College up in a neck of the woods in Seneca County" in New York, demanded that his students develop calluses on their hands, and "real sweat instead of mere perspiration." His statement that when he looked for books on agriculture in the Iowa State College library he might as well have sought cranberries in the Rocky Mountains is an indictment. But it indicts the library, or his own capacity for searching, not the fairly rich extant literature.[34]

The first agricultural teacher of scientific stature shortly appeared at Berkeley in Eugene Woldemar Hilgard, a pupil of Liebig's who came from Heidelberg by way of the University of Mississippi. It was his tactful exposition of soil chemistry that conquered the hostility of agrarian groups still ready to rip the college of agriculture out of the University of California. One keen observer of the speech he made to an audience of suspicious landholders in 1874 writes that the moment he arose, his deference, his anxiety to learn, and his reliance upon the help of the plain people, charmed everyone. Avoiding pedantry, he talked of soils like a farmer, not a scientist. Yet he was obviously so expert that questions came eagerly from all over the hall. An opposition leader, known for his ability to damn the classics all around a thousand-acre farm, suddenly leaned over to a friend to whisper: "My God, that man knows something." What he knew was Davy, Liebig, and their best American disciples. His biographer writes:

A single significant token of his victory may be seen in the fact that within five years of his coming, the State Master of the organization which set itself and its ten thousand members to the task of segregation of the College of Agriculture from the University pre-

[34] Isaac Phillips Roberts' rough-hewn, honest *Autobiography of a Farm Boy* (1916) describes how courageously he faced up to the task of teaching agriculture at Cornell when it was still regarded as "a school where hayseeds and greasy mechanics were taught to hoe potatoes, pitch manure, and be wet-nurses to steam engines."

sented, in the constitutional convention of 1879, the article which made the organic act of the University a part of the constitution of the State, and thus lifted the integrity of the institution above legislative dismemberment.

This achievement was . . . wide-reaching, for it has proved a rock upon which efforts for dismemberment of land-grant universities in other States have been dashed to pieces.[35]

When a proper organization of agricultural instruction took place, it was at the hands of men like Hilgard of California, Liberty Hyde Bailey of Cornell, and George Morrow of Illinois, who were both trained scientists and practical farmers. The teachers had to hammer into form courses in such totally unexplored areas as farm economics. Only men of imagination, scientific grounding, and energy could do it. The great lack was not of ideas or fragmentary science, but of personnel. That had been the chief want in Europe, where agricultural schools like those at Leipzig and Hohenheim in Germany had held precarious positions, and Rothamsted in England had confined itself to research without teaching. The emerging leaders who crystallized agricultural instruction were usually men of breadth like Hilgard, who read nine languages. Some of them were poets like Philip J. Bailey, who put his feeling for tillage into verse and essays. "To want a garden," he wrote, "is to be interested in plants, in the winds and rains, in birds and insects, in the warm-smelling earth." Few men have been as truly creative as Seaman A. Knapp, who began his colossal labors at Ames in 1879.

The land-grant institutions, combining old-style literary instruction with the new agricultural and mechanical departments, were like the partnership of Don Quixote and Sancho Panza. They quarreled abominably, but they aided

[35] Wickson, *E. W. Hilgard.*

each other more than they knew. It was fortunate that Sancho Panza, the industrial courses, took vigor so slowly. Had these courses been aggressively powerful, they might have crowded classical and scientific work out of some colleges. It was fortunate too that Sancho Panza held tenaciously to his rights, for when the 1880's and 1890's brought a crowd of new social and economic problems, Don Quixote needed help in grasping their importance.

V

The first quarter-century of the land-grant institutions illustrated all the faults and shortcomings of American democracy. They illustrated its impatience, eagerness for quick results, and proneness to believe that high objects might be achieved without arduous sacrifice. Our democracy preferred to have quick jerry-built fabrics rather than wait for substantial structures. It was full of veering crosswinds of opinion and complaint. Going West in 1872 to become president of the University of California, Daniel Coit Gilman paused in Urbana to discuss with Drs. Gregory and Shattuck the difficulties of the proper conduct of state institutions "amid unreasonable demands and clamors." They had much to discuss. This quarter-century revealed the democratic tendency toward disorderliness even at points where order was imperative. Military instruction, for example, an unpopular branch imposed by law, was an especially chaotic area, marked by fumbling half-starts. Our democratic love of enterprise and innovation was shown in the ready admission of women. The earliest large university to welcome them was Michigan, where the first woman to enter was so brilliant that she was at once promoted to the sophomore class. A number of land-grant institutions took them almost from the start. At the same time, democratic dislike of plan was revealed in the tardiness with which specific courses for women in home economics were devised.

Yet the land-grant colleges and state universities showed also the virtues of democracy. They illustrated its optimism, its idealism, its egalitarian passion, its readiness to take risks, and its liking for courageous action. The undertakings that the Morrill Act warmed into life were for the most part happy adventures. Hard as the struggle sometimes was, it had its exhilarations. The men who revitalized old institutions like Indiana and Wisconsin, who kept alive struggling seats like Louisiana and Georgia, and who founded new universities like those in Illinois, Nebraska, and Kansas, knew they were following the one possible course.

Theoretically, they could have avoided errors had they conserved land and money, delayed teaching until sure of a sound faculty and well-schooled student body, and waited to get decent libraries and laboratories. In so doing, they would have made the one really unforgivable error; they would have failed the young people asking help. As it was, they set to work with poor funds, poor teachers, poor buildings, and poor support — and they began training the talent that the young, fast-growing country desperately needed. They might have tried to place themselves above democracy, setting standards as yet above its reach; by the course they took they knit themselves into its very fiber. They knew that the coming decades were with them.

These institutions were evocative. They illustrated the fact that although democracy is supposed to begin at the bottom and grow upward, it can often begin at the top and pull the bottom to it. They also proved anew the fact that a great need can often raise up a man to meet it. Michigan and Cornell had the benefit of strong leaders in Angell and White from the Civil War onward, and both Wisconsin and California soon found one. It was Minnesota, however, which provided the most spectacular demonstration of what a determined man could accomplish. That university, when the Morrill Act passed, was seemingly moribund — some thought it already dead. It was practically without teachers, students, or hope when a self-made Yankee businessman of Minneapolis, John Pillsbury, stepped upon the scene. He sold hardware, and he came first to collect a bill of $1,000 for materials used in erecting the single building. He remained to rescue the institution.

A friend of the university devised a masterstroke to intercept Pillsbury's projected suit for collection of his debt. He induced the governor to offer Pillsbury a seat on the board of regents, persuaded Pillsbury to accept, and then helped the new officer to conceive an intense zeal for reviving the place. In all the annals of the state universities no story is more heroic than that of Pillsbury's battle in 1862-67 to make a university endowment out of a pile of debts; to make a university plant out of one dilapidated structure that had been used for a time to shelter livestock; and to make a student body out of groups of lads and girls hardly equipped to enter high school. Once Pillsbury's chief lieutenant told him the undertaking was hopeless. His reply was a grunt of five words: "I'm still not giving up."

And then suddenly, under the clear Minnesota skies, beside Minnehaha Falls, success bloomed like a sunflower. Pillsbury sliced the debts to a fraction of their face value and settled them. The legislature responded by appropriating $15,000 for a new start. An alert principal, W. W. Washburne, opened the preparatory school with thirty students. And in 1867 Pillsbury by a magnificent stroke captured the Morrill land grant of 120,000 acres by the simple expedient of annexing a purely paper project for a state agricultural college. To make good their title, the regents bought a tract of 120 acres between Minneapolis and St. Paul and dubbed it an experimental farm. It turned out to be too poor for farming, but eventually it was partitioned into residential sites at a useful profit. By 1875, thanks to the integrity, rich public spirit, and enterprise of the whilom debt collector, the University of Minnesota was now well launched on its career.

A decade later, in 1885, nearly all the land-grant institutions and state universities were well launched; the Hatch Act, for which Seaman A. Knapp of Iowa State had cleared the way, was about to give many of them the stimulus of another federal grant; and a second Morrill Act was not far away.[36] The best of them would soon enter upon a phase of assured greatness, ready to challenge the oldest and richest universities of the country.

[36] Morrill, who lived until December 28, 1899, took pride in introducing into the Senate his second educational act, under which the government pays $25,000 annually to each of the land-grant institutions. The Hatch Act of 1887, named for Representative William H. Hatch of Missouri, gave every state $15,000 annually for an agricultural research or experiment station in each land-grant college. This stimulated large state appropriations for the purpose. Quite as important, it opened an era of active cooperation between the colleges of agriculture and the Department of Agriculture.

THE FOOD

OF THE GODS

WHEN WE look back to the infancy of the land-grant institutions and the Western state universities, it seems difficult to understand their position and problems. That world of the 1870's is too remote to be apprehended without prolonged immersion in the history of the time. When we look back to the early maturity of these seats of instruction, however, in the years around 1900, comprehension seems fairly easy. That was the world of our grandparents, or even our fathers and mothers. The period is not utterly strange; it seems merely quaint.

If we thus hark back to 1900 we find Harvard then the largest of our universities, with about 5,500 students. We find Columbia almost abreast of it in annual income, and surpassing all other institutions in the salary scale of the faculty; professors there were paid from $5,000 to $7,500 a year, as against $5,000 at Johns Hopkins, $4,000 at Harvard, and $3,000 at Yale and the better state universities.[1] We find that German ideals in education still held a dominant repute, although some educators admired the English

[1] Curti and Carstensen, *Wisconsin,* I, 593, 594n.

tutorial system, and many applauded the English emphasis on extension teaching. To Andrew D. White, James B. Angell, Edmund J. James, and Benjamin Ide Wheeler, all of whom had studied in Germany, the Prussian university system seemed the best, and when Abraham Flexner published his book entitled *Universities* he ratified the verdict. We find that professors in those days universally worked hard. The eminent Moses Coit Tyler at Cornell, for example, had given ten hours a week to lectures and six to seminars, while eighteen hours was not uncommon for younger teachers. But these were the days of so much sport and diversion in the richer Eastern schools that Woodrow Wilson was presently to say: "So far as the colleges go, the sideshows have swallowed up the circus."

Actually, of course, the period was not quaint at all. It would be more accurate to say that both in America at large and in her universities, the Age of Innocence was ending and the Age of Realism was being born. Nowhere was it more fully accepted than in the land-grant and state universities, which did most to justify Lord Bryce's observation that while the universities of Germany were popular but not free, and the universities of England were free but not popular, those of America were both popular and free. We might add that the state universities were peculiarly individualistic, competitive, and attached to the idea of a free and mobile order. A majority of Americans, especially in the West, never forgot their theoretical faith in education as a national equalizer and still more as a preservative of an open society. Whether they had a truly realistic belief in equality is doubtful; they wished by personal success to establish inequality. But, we repeat, they emphatically believed that opportunity should be general, that everyone should be able to train whatever talents he possessed, and that all should have a chance to rise as far as their capacities permitted. Higher education safeguarded the social mobility of the nation, and that was the heart of democracy.

In their general ideology the state universities and land-grant colleges of this era and later were supporters neither of extreme radicalism nor of extreme conservatism. Most faculty members would have said that their ideology was separable from that of the general public only in being somewhat more advanced, and that they presented about the same spectrum of opinion as the general population.

They had been founded as expressions of the aspiring intellectual tradition in a democratic society; as agencies embodying the optimistic belief of the people in progress, their sense that their culture and economy are plastic, and their conviction that they ought constantly to transform and renovate their social environment. They were conservative in regarding property rights as inextricably mingled with human rights, and in accepting the basic Anglo-Saxon principle of compromise. They were radical in that they sharply questioned some of the values of the existing social system, now and then produced teachers who questioned them in the most sweeping fashion, and defended the right of these teachers to be heard. In central intent and character, however, they could best be called liberal as Mill or Woodrow Wilson would have used that term. As the greatest strength of the state universities was found west of the Alleghenies, and as the West during 1880-1920 had less property and more agrarian and Progressive ideas than the East, their liberalism was advanced in about the same degree as that of the people supporting them. E. Benjamin Andrews, resigning as head of Brown University when his trustees became hostile, found a friendly reception as head of Nebraska. No more than endowed universities, however, did they let liberalism run into revolutionary radicalism. Even Thomas Jefferson, in stocking the University of Virginia with professors, had been unable to carry the heterodox Thomas Cooper within its doors; even John Bascom would not have proposed Henry George for a chair. The state universities were practical in their dominant sociopolitical attitudes. They held with Burke: "Abstract liberty, like other abstractions, is not to be found."

Faculties and presidents, in their liberal position, were generally ready to endorse the statement made by Lotus D. Coffman at Minnesota that "the schools of democracy are not forums for the spread of doctrine" and that classrooms should not be "arenas for the promotion of any particular social theories." At the same time, they realized that the object in education is not to make ideas safe for students, but to make students safe for ideas, and that the clash of ideas, from Platonism to Marxism, lies at the root of true instruction. An Ely or a Veblen was not to be silenced; he was to be encouraged.

I

Within the academic world there were three principal changes, reflecting not only modern developments of knowledge but also the effort to guard against stratification and keep our society open and free. The first was the growing specialization of university work to furnish professional preparation, in scores of fields, to meet the specialization of American life. New courses from ceramics to social psychology blossomed in the curricula. The "mechanic arts" or engineering studies were compartmentalized into numerous quite distinct callings. Pure science demanded not one department and faculty, but a variety. In the social studies one new organization after another testified to the reorganization of knowledge in expert divisions: the American Historical Association in 1884, the American Economic Association in 1885, the American Political Science Association in 1904, the American Sociological Society in 1905, and the American Statistical Association and American Anthropological Association soon after.

The state and land-grant universities were to a special degree seats of professional specialization; and they gave the son of the poorest artisan or tenant farmer opportunity to rise to professional heights in law, medicine, or any other occupation. Yet as most of them were outside large population centers, they aften retained, as Edwin E. Slosson observed, more unity than the equally specialized Harvard or Columbia. At Illinois a humanist eagerly took Slosson to view the agricultural research work; in Berkeley a scientist lamented that the visitor was just too late to see classic drama in the Greek theater. Still, all universities had problems of integration.

The second important response to the realism of the time was a greater concentration in teaching upon thought and analysis, and a diminished emphasis on desiccated fact. Rote instruction as known in the 1860's was dead. The ever greater complexity and interconnection of social problems made the old approach to life by memorization of packets of knowledge impossible. The essential aim was to prepare the student mind to wrestle with these complexities. And the third response to the new era was an enhanced earnestness among students and teachers alike. This was particularly visible west of the Alleghenies, where it helped atone for the manifest academic handicaps of the region. Jane Addams illustrates it when she writes that as she and her Rockford College friends neared the end of their course, "we avowed eternal allegiance to 'our ideals,' and promised each other that we would 'never abandon them without conscious self-justification.' "

In 1907 two curious episodes apprised the country that the state universities had gained national acceptance as adult institutions, dignified in their standards. William Trufant Foster of Bowdoin that spring wrote a public letter protesting against an appropriation which the legislature had just given the University of Maine for its college of liberal arts. Maine's land-grant college, he argued, had at first confined itself to agriculture and technology. Later, growing into a university, it had embraced forestry, pharmacy, education, and law. But to proceed now to teach liberal arts was an egregious wrong. Three older seats, Bowdoin, Bates, and Colby, fully supplied the needs of Maine youth. It would be impossible, Foster declared, to tack liberal arts courses of genuine merit to a program of industrial studies. Let Maine use the money instead to improve her primary schools![2]

To this attack a crushing response was at once made by a North Carolina educator who had come north to Wesleyan College in Connecticut. The opposition of denominational colleges to state universities, he pointed out, once strong in parts of the South and West, was virtually dead. This was because such opposition was futile; because the rise of the state universities to greatness — and some were great indeed — had plainly benefited, not hurt, the endowed colleges; and because liberal people comprehended the wis-

[2] *The Nation,* vol. 84, May 2, 1907.

dom of meeting Justin S. Morrill's stipulation that the land-grant institutions be not merely technical but also liberal. Inquiry would show, he asserted, that the University of Maine already provided a liberal arts instruction quite equaling that at Bowdoin, Bates, and Colby. He might have added that Foster's letter was read with stupefaction in the West, where people in the shadow of the growing state universities could not believe that opinion could be so archaic, even at Bowdoin.

Simultaneously, President Hadley of Yale made a stir by a speech declaring that the student constituency of the Western universities was provincial and local compared with that of their Eastern sisters. Upon this taunt President Angell of Michigan promptly brought down a sledge-hammer contradiction. The latest catalogues of Yale and the University of Michigan showed that while both took students from every state and territory, Michigan took them from a larger number of the insular dependencies. Michigan also had students from a larger number of foreign countries and provinces than Yale. Moreover, with every one of the New England states well represented at Ann Arbor, Michigan enrolled far more students from the other Midwestern states than did Yale. The truth is, wrote Angell, that "there are several western universities whose constituency is quite as cosmopolitan as that of their Eastern rivals."[3]

In both East and West, university standards even in 1910 still left a great deal to be desired. Barrett Wendell of Harvard had just declared: "College education is today chiefly notable for its ineffectiveness." The same opinion had been expressed in two noteworthy books by Clarence Birdseye and Dr. Abraham Flexner. Although secondary schools had

[3] *The Nation,* vol. 84, May 16, 1907.

multiplied, and although a wider range of admission subjects made failure every year less excusable, a majority of
entrants into universities everywhere failed to meet the stip-
ulated requirements. The indulgent academic authorities
let them in anyway. "We allow you," they said in effect, "to
try to do college work in the same classes with those who are
truly prepared, and in addition, require you to make up
your deficiencies."

Harvard College said this in 1908-09 to 58 per cent of its
607 freshmen. Yale said it that year to 57 per cent of its in-
coming class. Columbia College said it to about the same
proportion, and indeed, admitted nineteen freshmen who
were deficient by a full year of preparatory work. Princeton
in 1908 admitted 301 out of 360 freshmen with conditions.
So true was it then, as earlier and later, that the high
schools were the weakest link in the nation's educational
chain.

It must be admitted that land-grant standards of admission were almost universally lower than those of the best
endowed institutions, and in some places were abysmally
low. Thus as late as 1900 the Georgia State College of Agriculture and the Mechanic Arts had almost no entrance requirements at all. Any student could enter who presented
elementary English, and mathematics through three books
of geometry. The bars were let down because Georgia had
distressingly few high schools. In 1904, in fact, Chancellor
Walter B. Hill of the University of Georgia reported that
the high schools of the state, so far as he had been able to
find, were graduating only about 350 students. Half of the
students would stop at that point. All the higher educational
institutions of Georgia thus had to scramble for the other
175 students who chose to seek college training inside the

state.[4] The University of Missouri at this time admitted to its agricultural courses anybody who offered one unit of English, one of algebra, and one in any other subject. Though poor secondary preparation was the rule from the Atlantic to the Pacific, the state universities in particular had to cling overlong to their preparatory departments, meanwhile striving to help develop decent high school systems by the use of inspectors and rules of accreditation.

Nevertheless, it could be said by 1900, and still more by 1910, that the better land-grant institutions and state universities had arrived at a position of maturity. In the latter year Edwin E. Slosson, publishing his book *Great American Universities,* gave the distinction of that title to eight endowed institutions and six state or land-grant institutions, the six being Michigan, Cornell, Minnesota, Wisconsin, California, and Illinois. The Carnegie Foundation for the Advancement of Teaching had made the same list. The privately endowed universities ran back to 1636, but the new public institutions, born mainly since 1862, would soon be running neck and neck with them. However, they must rise to greatness in their own way, not as merely imitative institutions.

II

President John Bascom had struck a challenging note in his report to the Wisconsin regents when he retired in 1887. "The University of Wisconsin," he declared, "is in that transitional period when it is easy to go either forward or backward." He knew whereof he spoke. Unless the state universities converted the public to a fuller support and extended their functions both in height and in area, after 1887 they might really have slipped backward. Instead, they

[4] Brooks, *Georgia Under Sixteen Administrations,* 117, 118.

went forward. The chief problems in the years of their founding had been to strike root into their states, to find students even if they had to prepare many students themselves, and to establish a workable balance among humanistic, scientific, and industrial studies. Now, having accomplished this by 1887 or thereabouts, the leading public universities had to go much further.

Specifically, they had to achieve three great objectives. Their primary task was to develop a character all their own, so well adapted to their environment that everybody could see that the land-grant college or university was a unique institution, thoroughly characteristic of its own society. Their second goal was to make themselves broadly useful to their states, not merely in traditional avenues but in many new ways, becoming, in the term invented by an English university leader, "community service centers." The third and most difficult objective was to gain some of the distinction that men had associated with universities ever since medieval Bologna and Paris flourished, and in so doing to lift both the intellectual and spiritual level of democracy.

Inevitably, the movement forward in the years from 1890 to 1920 was uneven. We seem justified in saying that the University of Michigan led the march, as it had done ever since it outstripped the University of Virginia in ante bellum days. Midway between East and West, it combined some of the best traits of both sections, uniting progressivism with sound traditional standards. Cornell under Andrew D. White made a record quite as distinguished, but not as clearly identified with the growth of the state. Two other institutions could feel warm pride in the scope, thoroughness, and originality of their work: California and Wisconsin. The remainder marched at irregular distances behind, fired by the example of the first four but constrained to keep pace with their people. As Dr. Slosson remarked, the Universities of Illinois and Minnesota were just emerging in 1910 from adolescence to manhood. They were like overgrown youths whose clothes were too small, whose control over their limbs and voices was erratic, and who had not yet decided whether to be preacher, ranchman, or locomotive engineer.[5]

The advance of the universities was uneven primarily because uneveness, materially and culturally, characterized the progress of their states. Michigan moved faster than Indiana, and Illinois faster than Missouri. Special circumstances, sometimes quite fortuitous, also affected the rate of progress. It is difficult to understand why the people of Illinois for the quarter-century from 1869 to 1894 were so apathetic about their university. Finally the establishment of the University of Chicago by John D. Rockefeller and the election of Altgeld as governor so awakened them that a new president, Andrew Sloan Draper, found Springfield far more sympathetic than it had ever been before. The unfortunate early name, Illinois Industrial University, the long agricultural depression, and the divergence between Chicago and downstate interests perhaps help explain the retardation. The Universities of Missouri, Tennessee, and Arkansas had to take heavy buffets in the stormy years of Civil War and Reconstruction, and necessarily shared state poverty. The University of Kansas and Kansas State College suffered from the political and social turbulence which William Allen White denounced in his famous editorial, "What's the Matter with Kansas?"

How hard the struggle in some states was may be

[5] Edwin E. Slosson, *Great American Universities* (1910), 250.

gathered from the history of Louisiana State University under its first president, David F. Boyd, who if neither the ablest nor the most famous of land-grant leaders was surely the most heroic. Boyd, a graduate of the University of Virginia and a major in the Confederate army, became head of the Louisiana State Seminary a few months after Appomattox, and remained with the institution, long its chief and always its animating spirit, until his death in 1899. He was spared no ordeal and no indignity from political upheaval to private insult, from bitter hatred to neglect and destitution. He triumphed over all his trials with a gallantry that should be better known outside Louisiana.

Meanwhile, at a happier extreme, the University of Michigan was fortunate not only in the thirty-year administration of the statesmanlike James Burrill Angell, but also in a well-established tradition of state pride in the work at Ann Arbor. Wisconsin profited from the fact that a roster of loyal sons, including such political opposites as John C. Spooner and Robert M. La Follette, became prominent state leaders at an early period.[6] The University of Minnesota found Yankee, German, and Scandinavian settlers rallying to its side; and Michigan State and Iowa State produced two leaders of rare quality in Kenyon L. Butterfield and Seaman A. Knapp — men more than leaders, for both were creators.

No story in university annals is more inspiring than Boyd's battle to keep what is now Louisiana State University alive after the war, nursing it through bankruptcy, the political

[6] Robert M. La Follette in the first chapter of his *Autobiography* (1913) describes his debt to the University of Wisconsin. His old teacher John Bascom gave him a piece of advice when he became governor that he always treasured: "Robert, you will doubtless make mistakes of judgment as governor, but never mind the political mistakes so long as you make no ethical mistakes."

banditries of Reconstruction, and the enmity of white voters resentful of carpetbagger laws which compelled the admission of Negro students. The slender public allowances were paid in almost worthless paper. One year no appropriation was made at all. "This day," Boyd wrote in his diary, July 23, 1847, "finds our poor school in very bad condition, terribly in debt, ourselves so poor that we are in actual want — no money and no credit — and the impression pretty general throughout Louisiana that the University cannot stand." For three years he had bought no clothes for himself and his large family, wearing his Confederate coat because he had no other. As Christmas approached he wrote that many a time recently the household had been doubtful of food one or two days ahead, and "even sometimes of a morning we did not know that we would have anything for dinner."

Yet although the student body once fell to four, Boyd kept the banner flying. His labors effected in 1877 a merger of the state university and the Agricultural and Mechanical College, the university turning over to the new institution just $4.17 in cash. He gathered together a few well-trained professors: one a former teacher at Princeton and Columbia, one a Michigan graduate who later became president of Washington State University, and one a cultivated son of the poet Richard Henry Wilde. Indeed, Walter L. Fleming tells us that under Boyd, Louisiana probably had the best faculty in the South. He made the most of the hundred-acre campus that Baton Rouge presented the university. He gradually strengthened the pitiful library. Removed from the presidency in 1880, he was unanimously reelected in 1884, only to be removed again a little later; yet when he died at the end of the century, he was still an active professor in the institution he had helped organize forty years earlier.[7]

No other state university or land-grant college owed more to a single man. As a colleague said when a memorial hall was dedicated in his honor, his selfless devotion must always inspire the youth of Louisiana to higher standards of conduct, for "he founded a great university without money and endowed it with his radiant soul."

The first great objective, we have said, was to establish an individual character, a distinctive personality; and this was unquestionably achieved by the land-grant and other public institutions, taken as a whole, before 1910. As Slosson wrote, all state universities by that time looked alike to Eastern men, just as Yale, Harvard, and Princeton looked alike to westerners. What was the character and how was it formed?

Benjamin Ide Wheeler of California took some pains to answer these questions. The principal contrast between the old endowed seats of learning and the publicly supported universities lay, he observed in one of his essays, in a "marked difference of atmosphere," which was produced by various elements. These elements, according to President Wheeler, were first, co-education; second, engineering and applied science, subjects which he thought raised standards of hard work but crucified the imagination; third, agriculture, "which leaves the door open and lets the cold air in"; fourth, the exclusion of church or chapel, for state institutions had to avoid entanglements with dogma; fifth, compulsory drill, a useful discipline where so little else was compulsory; and sixth, the absence of a robust tuition charge. This was a fairly sound list, so far as it went, al-

[7] Fleming, *Louisiana State University*, 255-260.

though it ignored the fact that coeducation was slowly becoming universal, and it exaggerated the exclusion of religion. It also omitted two salient differentiating elements; the work of the state universities in distributing information and ideas to the whole public, chiefly in the extension activities which they carried much further than the endowed universities; and the strong link between the state universities and the high schools which they inspected and partly guided.[8]

Most important of all, President Wheeler's list omitted the fact that the state university atmosphere derived an idiosyncratic quality from the state itself. This was a subtle entity, to be defined only by those who drew the atmosphere into their lungs: by people like William Allen White, who was at the University of Kansas in 1888, and Willa Cather, graduated from the University of Nebraska in 1895, and Carleton H. Parker, graduated from California at Berkeley in 1904, and Carl Van Doren, graduated from Illinois in 1908, and Henry A. Wallace, graduated from Iowa State College in 1910, and James W. Fulbright, graduated from the University of Arkansas in 1925, and Ralph Bunche, graduated from California at Los Angeles in 1927. It was a dull student who did not derive a certain largeness of view and sense of civic responsibility from the way in which so many interests of the commonwealth centered in the university. That at any rate Willa Cather makes us feel in her novel of the University of Nebraska, *One of Ours*. The atmosphere, according to some critics, was a bit too earthy, too utilitarian, and too expansive, but those qualities certainly did not dominate the careers of the persons just listed.

[8] See Benjamin Ide Wheeler's book of addresses and essays, *The Abundant Life* (1924).

Under favorable circumstances, pragmatism and idealism merged for the best students in a sense of identity with the state. President Wheeler, who was head of California for the first twenty years of the century, remarked that the alumni of the state universities felt too little gratitude to their alma mater. Whereas the son of an endowed seat often said, "What can I do for my university?" the state university graduate asked, "What can I get out of my university?" This, assuredly, is most unjust. Dr. Wheeler overlooks the fact that graduates were naturally grateful to the state rather than to its academic child.

What the best of them — Robert M. La Follette, William Allen White, Henry Wallace, and James W. Fulbright — certainly said was, "What can I do for my state?" To many the university, the state, and the idea of service all merged into an appeal to their loyalties which a Pennsylvanian going to Harvard, or a Carolinian attending Princeton, could never feel. It was said that to hear President George E. Vincent begin an address to his students with the words, "Men of Minnesota!" was, to a youth from St. Paul or Gopher Prairie, to experience the emotion of an ancient Roman as, drawing his toga about him, he announced: "Civis Romanus sum!"[9] The people of Kansas, as Carl Becker tells us, felt a spirit all their own from the days of John Brown. The Californians had their peculiar spirit from the time of Starr King and Bret Harte, and the Illinoisians felt theirs from the era of Lincoln and Douglas. The greater

[9] Gray, *Minnesota*, 151. Vincent had an inspirational quality that sometimes seemed "more than human splendor." But Guy Stanton Ford (Gray, *Minnesota*, 148) founded the assertion that Vincent effected a second founding of the university upon the fact that he "knit a loose federation of disparate colleges into a self-conscious, cooperating, and purposeful institution of higher learning."

state universities by 1910 were instilling a comprehension of this special spirit into their children.

III

The most distinctive characteristic of the state institutions in this period, however, was something very different: it was their heavy emphasis, as before noted, upon professional training. Many of them in the years 1890-1930 became primarily congeries of professional schools, which they created to satisfy public demand. The pattern of action followed in most instances was simple and natural. A new vocation or new purpose would arise; its adherents would say to themselves, "Why should we not have a school of our own at the university?"; they would bring appropriate pressures to bear; and lo, as a result of external rather than internal initiative, the school would spring into being.

Thus in 1883 a new regent of the University of California, Arthur Rodgers, used a commencement address to call attention to the vast commerce with the Orient that California, emulating the Portuguese, Dutch, and British, might develop. The result was the opening at Berkeley in 1898 of the first university college of commerce in the country. In Missouri George S. Johns, editor of the St. Louis *Post-Dispatch,* in 1906 invited a student group to write, edit, and produce a special Sunday section. The experiment attracted so much attention that Missouri newspapermen called for a school of journalism; and this duly began work under Dean Walter Williams in 1908, four years before the Pulitzer School in Columbia University opened. Requests from three Midwestern railroads, including the Illinois Central, led the University of Illinois to institute transportation courses while they were hardly known elsewhere. Since New York state was a primary center of electrical development, Cornell very properly opened advanced courses and granted the world's first doctorate in electrical engineering in 1886.[10]

Agriculture in these years fully established itself as what Dr. Gregory in 1870 had asserted it was not: a science, and hence a profession. The passage of the Hatch Act in 1887 marked its emergence into that status. No longer did men have to talk of Rothamsted in discussing agricultural research — they had better examples at home; no longer was the study a stepchild. Liberty Hyde Bailey, visiting a prosperous farm home, once heard the parents of a bright boy discussing where he should go to college. The mother remarked: "His father wants him to go to an agricultural college, but I want him to get an education." The date of the clear emergence of agriculture as a profession might well be fixed in January, 1893, when Bailey addressed his students and colleagues at Cornell on "Agricultural Education and its Place in the University Curriculum." The time had passed, he said, for lumping together all agricultural instruction under one or two professors, and it must thenceforth be scientifically systematized in a number of categories. Spe-

[10] See Viles, *Missouri;* Walter Williams, *The Practise of Journalism* (1911); W. W. Ferrier, *Origin . . . of the University of California;* Nevins, *Illinois,* 181. But in some striking instances, the inspiration for a new course or school of professional study came from an academic leader, not an economic group or other special interest. In some instances it came from a figure in the state or federal government. The first real forestry school in the country, the New York State College of Forestry at Cornell, was born in 1898 mainly as a result of the activities of Bernhard E. Fernow, chief of the forestry division in the national Department of Agriculture, of Liberty Hyde Bailey in the university, and of an alert governor. See Fernow's *A Brief History of Forestry* (1911).

cialized teaching and research were needed in dairying, field crops, horticulture, forestry, animal husbandry, and other areas. While standard courses in botany, chemistry, and geology were useful, "the indispensable and vital part of agricultural teaching is agriculture."[11]

Men were already acting upon the principles which Bailey laid down. When Eugene Davenport came to Illinois under President Draper, the university had but one professorship of agriculture. He rejected this title, insisted on calling himself professor of animal husbandry, organized instruction in agronomy, dairy husbandry, and horticulture as well, brought in Cyril G. Hopkins to assist him, and induced T. J. Burrill to lend a hand. By 1900 he had twelve faculty members giving seventy-five courses, and two years later, twenty-four men giving about 100 courses. Illinois then offered the broadest range of agricultural instruction in America.

At Minnesota Dean Albert F. Woods, accomplishing a similar reorganization, scored by 1907 what the university historian calls an "enormous success." At Missouri a native farm-bred teacher who had studied in Leipzig and Zurich, Henry J. Waters, assembled a vigorous faculty and carried through the same work. One of his staff, Frederick B. Mumford, won national fame in animal husbandry. The reconstitution of the agricultural work at Wisconsin under Dean William A. Henry similarly involved the assemblage of a versatile faculty, including the first agricultural physicist known to any university. Here Dr. Stephen W. Babcock invented a quick and accurate method of measuring the butterfat of milk. "The Babcock test," said Dean Henry, "was

[11] A. D. Rodgers, *Liberty Hyde Bailey* (1949), 186-241.

to associated [cooperative] dairying what the Morse electric telegraph was to railroad operation."

The state and land-grant universities meanwhile led the entire country in the professional diversification of technology. Civil engineering, mechanical engineering, electrical engineering, sanitary engineering, ceramic engineering, aeronautical engineering, and other professional courses emerged one by one. The public universities found their establishment of these courses facilitated by their close relations with industry and their ability to recruit eager high school graduates. One of the historians of Harvard comments: "In the period 1871-1890, when other institutions, having lower requirements for admission, were providing instruction in new fields of engineering as they developed, no such expansion took place in the [Harvard] school." Indeed, Harvard lost ground when it abandoned mining engineering to the Universities of Michigan, Minnesota, and California. The state institutions became the principal cradle of the new technological professions.

It was plain that as state activities and needs increased, professional work would inevitably keep pace. Eventually hotel keeping in New York, wine making in California, and automotive design in Michigan would all have their well-organized courses. The library schools of Michigan and Illinois gained special distinction, and after 1900 schools of education and of business drew impressive registrations everywhere. This accentuation of functional activities inevitably affected curriculum and teaching methods in all parts of the larger state universities. Even instruction in Elizabethan literature and Hegelian philosophy became tinged by the practical approach. It tended, writes Edward D. Eddy, "to make the liberal arts generally less formal and other-worldly, and consequently more related to the immediate needs of the students and of modern life."[12]

Naturally, many professors of the humanities viewed this tendency with a certain misgiving. We find a teacher of English at Wisconsin acidly observing that service to a fellow man could as well lie in presenting him with a more just concept of values in art or morals as in enlarging his philosophy of municipal sewage. When the president of Wisconsin remarked in 1904 that the college of agriculture had increased state wealth by ten or twenty times the amount of the state appropriations, some teachers saw a lurking danger in the statement. It was easy to discern what Babcock's milk test did for the lacteal economy; it was not so easy to see that Frederick Jackson Turner's essay of the same year on the significance of the frontier did more for the world reputation of Wisconsin than all the feats of the college of agriculture.

Always and everywhere, the responsiveness of state universities to popular interests tended to pull them into im-

[12] Stuart P. Sherman wrote in *The Genius of America* (1923) that when legislators came to apportion money to the state universities, they said a great deal about agriculture, engineering, and business, and little about literature. This, he argued, was entirely wrong, for literature was the vehicle of the most potent ideas, and the crystallization of the best social convictions. From Aeschuylus to Ruskin it has been one of the most formidable powers in human affairs. "Literature is the effective voice of the social government." But we must add that the more practical departments of the greater state universities have always been deferential to the liberal arts departments, and that this deference has grown. The separate agricultural and engineering colleges down to 1920 paid just enough attention to liberal arts to save themselves from becoming mere trade schools. Since that date the best have paid a good deal more, though as Eddy says (*Colleges for Our Land and Time*, 215, 216), their literary departments "have been more valuable historically for what they have prevented than for what they have produced."

balance. Perhaps the imbalance created by professionalism had a temporary justification in promoting an open society. Perhaps, also, it was less serious than it seemed. Aeschuylus, Shakespeare, and Goethe might be crowded out of the engineering schools, but not out of the institution as a whole. It was a happy fact that most university presidents continued to be men reared in the liberal tradition. Charles Kendall Adams, who held sway over two academic seats in turn, was a historian; Benjamin Ide Wheeler was a professor of Greek; Charles R. Van Hise was a geologist; George E. Vincent had been literary editor of the Chautauqua Press; Edmund J. James was an economist. Martin Kellogg, who became head of the University of California in 1893, had taught the ancient classics. In his inaugural he roundly declared that many minds had been trained for greatness under the classic disciplines. "The subjects taught in former generations," he went on, "are not at all effete; we cannot afford to despise the knowledge and literature of former ages. . . . Our university . . . must gather up the treasures of the past, and add them to the fast-accumulating treasures of the present."

The second main objective of the state and land-grant universities was, as we have said, to make themselves broadly useful not only in traditional but also in novel ways. James B. Angell, presiding at Ann Arbor for forty years, tells us that in considering the relation of the university to democracy he always kept two primary objects in view. "First, I have endeavored to induce every citizen to regard himself as a stockholder in the institution, who had a real interest in making it of the greatest service to his children. Secondly, I have sought to make all the schools and teachers in the State understand that they and the university are parts of one united system, and that therefore the youngest pupil in the most secluded schoolhouse should be encouraged to see that the path was open from his home up to and through the university."[13]

One of the best of the state university services in this period was assuredly the elevation of the high schools; a slow, uncertain, but still perceptible elevation. All over the republic university officers did their utmost to encourage backward villages to build high schools; they cheered on the ill-paid men and women, often but two or three to a school, who taught history and English without libraries and physics without apparatus; they insisted year by year on better standards. Wisconsin established a system of free high schools in 1875 and Minnesota in 1881, while other states kept pace; so that by 1914 the country boasted more than 11,500 public high schools with 58,000 teachers. Many of these high schools applied what William Torrey Harris of St. Louis termed the American idea in secondary education: "not what the teacher does for the pupil, but what he gets the pupil to do for himself, is of value." The state and land-grant institutions assuredly tried to inculcate this principle. They sent out lecturers who vitalized the local teachers' institutes that, as one of Henry Barnard's happy inspirations, had overspread the country. Where they could, they helped install work in manual arts, agriculture, and domestic science.

In time, most authorities accepted the principle that high school inspection is properly a function of the state department of education, not of the state university. But meanwhile a memorable work had been accomplished. When the

[13] Wilfred B. Shaw, *A Short History of the University of Michigan* (1934).

university system of accreditation came under attack in Wisconsin, a faculty committee made an able defensive report. That system lasted for more than a half-century, and under it more than 450 high schools won acceptable status. Each of these schools was visited by a university professor, sometimes almost annually, from the 1880's to 1931. The record was one of patient, laborious service. "In the early days the inspector often had to give a public lecture at the school to help pay his expenses. He had spent the day before or after the lecture visiting the high school classes, observing the teachers, and examining the courses of study. Upon returning to Madison, he had written his formal report to the University accrediting committee, and, to the superintendent of the school he had visited, a letter giving his observations, criticisms, and suggestions. If his report called for action, the committee had to meet, discuss the matter, and often present it to the faculty for final decision." Such a system was a mighty fulcrum in lifting secondary education, however painfully, to a more efficient level.[14]

IV

The four essential elements of university growth have always been men, money, freedom, and leadership. Men and money were now being more abundantly provided. Wisconsin's resounding assertion of academic freedom in 1894, a declaration that the faculty must be protected in the "fearless sifting and winnowing" of ideas, was profoundly felt almost everywhere. As for leadership, it was concentrated primarily in the presidents. That of the state university heads stopped at the state borders, while that of the best heads of endowed universities spread far afield. In the Mid-

[14] Curti and Carstensen, *Wisconsin,* II, 241-251.

west, William Rainey Harper of Chicago had a much broader impact on his section than even Van Hise or James; David Starr Jordan of Stanford had a similar potency in the far West; and Presidents Butler and Eliot exercised a truly national leadership. Still, many state institutions were ably guided.

In administration any foreign visitor might have concluded that public universities now and later, like other universities, were about as devoid of democracy as the Sahara is of water. Chancellor Samuel P. Capen of Buffalo, in his book *The Management of Universities,* termed them "a simon-pure example of authoritarian government." Their boards of trustees were in many instances responsible to nobody but themselves. Their presidents represented a massive concentration of executive power. In the English universities, especially of the Oxbridge type, the teachers exercise a direct authority over their own work and privileges. Actually, however, the American system as it now developed was far more democratic than it seemed; and for our society and environment, it was much more efficient than a copy of any European system could be. The functions of the boards of trustees were basically different from those of the boards of directors for General Motors or the Southern Pacific railroad. They acted as guardians, not governors; as caretakers, not managers. They did their proper work in advising, not ordering, in interpreting the university to the people and legislature, and in nourishing and defending it. The president meanwhile, in the internal administration of this simple period, found himself answerable to faculty senate and committees. What concentration of power he enjoyed did for the university much what presidential power did for the nation, facilitating plan, change, and progress.

He had to be executive officer for the trustees, head of the faculty, and petitioner to the legislature, a triple function which left him feeling far more servant than master.

In describing the breadth of democratic service by administrators, much might be said about the University of Missouri under Richard Henry Jesse, a Virginian who had taught Latin at Tulane but who took office in 1891 with a set of very twentieth-century reforms; about Michigan under the famous Dr. Angell; about California under Benjamin Ide Wheeler; about Illinois under the sagacious and lovable Edmund J. James; about Minnesota under the sturdy Cyrus Northrop; Nebraska under E. Benjamin Andrews; and a dozen other institutions and their heads from North Carolina to Oregon. It would be invidious to choose among them. No exception, however, can be taken to the choice for a brief special examination of the work done at Wisconsin under Charles R. Van Hise, for it was there and then that a land-grant university could first truly assert that "the borders of the campus are the boundaries of the State."

When the tall, lean, hawk-faced Van Hise, reared and trained in Wisconsin, became professor of geology in 1892, he was already a leader of rare personality. He had the endurance, drive, optimism, and practicality of the frontier. Yet he was an introvert, a thinker, who had agonized over his partial loss of religious faith, and who gave intense thought to first principles, on which he had a way of throwing out stimulating comment. "The man has not yet lived," he said, "who can adequately describe a grain of sand." Nor was his thinking and reading narrow. Science for him bore the closest relationship to history, sociology, economics, and letters. He found a congenial companion in his neighbor Frederick Jackson Turner, the two agreeing that physiography could not be understood without history, nor history without physiography, and sharing an enthusiasm for the writings of John Wesley Powell. Van Hise's associates noted his constant interest in theory and generalization, and his insistence that facts must continually be illumined by interpretation. He drove himself hard and expected students and staff to keep up. When somebody reported failure in an assigned task his stern lips and piercing blue-gray eyes conveyed a rebuke like a whiplash. He had his own definition for an excuse. It was, he said, "a reason for the happening of something which if it hadn't happened for that reason would have happened for some other."[15]

Van Hise brought to the presidency at Wisconsin, a post which he held from 1903 until his death in 1918, an array of strongly held ideas; but the chief one was the necessity for an identification of the state and its university in a wide range of activities. Faculty members, he insisted, should be efficient servants of the public, or leave; they should enjoy no protected status under the name of tenure. "Whether or not a man is retained in a faculty," he said, "should depend upon his capacity to meet his duty to the institution. There is no possible excuse for retaining on the staff of a university an inefficient man." In short, the university did not exist for the professors, but for the students who looked to it for food, and for the taxpayers who supported it.

Dominating the university throughout two decades, Van Hise made it famous and influential by his accentuation of

[15] William Ellery Leonard in a sonnet on Van Hise emphasized his scientific work and his zeal for university extension: "he built with faithful hands, new roads from hills of thought to humble hearts." Maurice M. Vance in *Charles Richard Van Hise* (1960) unites a personal portrait with a compact analysis of the man's accomplishments.

service to the commonwealth. Bryce one remarked that the chief glory of the University of Virginia was that "she has been a home of patriotism and civic virtue," and this could be as truly said of the University of Wisconsin. Van Hise thought it fortunate that the institution stood in the capital, so that teachers, legislators, and governor could better understand each other. He counted it fortunate, too, that the alumni numbered such able public servants as William F. Vilas, who entered Cleveland's cabinet and finally bequeathed his whole fortune of about three million dollars to the university; as Senator John C. Spooner; and as "Bob" La Follette, a fellow-student in old days with Van Hise. While he was governor, La Follette held a regular Saturday luncheon party of state officials, legislators, and faculty men. John Bascom had enunciated his hope that the university would become a vital force, not only in the material development of Wisconsin, but also in guiding its social, political, and intellectual life. But he merely pointed out the goal, whereas Van Hise planned and took the steps that achieved it.

He urged university men upon the state for expert tasks, and rejoiced when they were appointed. He liked nothing better than to undertake some state enterprise, and tell his colleagues — in a favorite phrase — "we must push it vigorously." Governor La Follette made the professor of transportation one of the three public utility commissioners. John R. Commons served in various capacities, notably as a member of the state industrial commission. Paul S. Reinsch, a specialist on the Far East, attended international conferences before he became ambassador to China. The state tax commission leaned heavily on the university experts. The fact that Wisconsin was long the only state to have an unemployment compensation law, of the type now universal, was partly attributable to the enlightenment shed by the university. When Dr. Slosson wished to talk with Professor Balthazar H. Meyer, he was told that Meyer was at the capitol presiding over the state railroad commission. When he went to the capitol he was told that Meyer was at the university holding a seminar. Slosson tried to find Charles McCarthy of the famous legislative reference bureau at his state office, and learned he was on the campus helping coach the football team.

All this work, it need not be said, was unselfishly done. When Commons finished organizing the state industrial commission, he resigned. He has decided, Van Hise announced, "that the State pays him so much that he cannot remain there, as he has not been able to discover a way to spend the $5,000 per annum that is paid to him; therefore he is returning to the university for $3,500."

And Van Hise became the most enthusiastic of the state university presidents over the value of extension teaching. He wanted no mute inglorious Milton in the state, he said; it should be the aim of extension to make this impossible, and at the same time to assist the multitude who fell short of Miltonic stature. It was William Rainey Harper of the University of Chicago who had first exhorted Van Hise to undertake energetic planning in this field. For a time the president had remained indifferent, but when Charles McCarthy reported in 1906 that 35,000 residents of Wisconsin were paying $800,000 a year for correspondence instruction, he awoke to the opportunity. Correspondence courses, lecture programs, study and debating groups, and a general information service were organized. Critics, of course, objected that such instruction was not of true university grade.

He met them with two answers: first, a great deal of it would be, and second, the university was the one agency of the state which could so embody the combined intellectual life of the community that it could apply that life on any level for the betterment of the community. Extension would truly convert the institution into a people's university, the old ideal of Jonathan B. Turner and Greeley, and it would truly give it, as a campus, the full state area of 56,000 square miles.

The success of Wisconsin's extension department, not only rapid but sustained, proved the soundness of Van Hise's judgment. He was able to assert in 1915 that during the previous year the university had devoted nearly twice as much money to extension as any other in the land. He had attained the objective which he early defined: "I shall never be content until the beneficent influence of the university reaches every home in the state." Many people then regarded Wisconsin as a radical community. Van Hise often said that its dependence on university experts in government proved it conservative, and he would have added that extension was a conservative effort to lift the general level of intelligence. By its broad-based activities the university became more than what William Hard called it, a consulting engineer in the life of the state. As Lincoln Steffens wrote in 1909:

> In Wisconsin the university is as close to the intelligent farmer as his pigpen or his toolhouse; the university laboratories are part of the alert manufacturer's plant; to the worker, the university is drawing nearer than the school around the corner, and is as much his as his union, or his favorite saloon. Creeping into the minds of the children with pure seed, into the debates of youth with pure facts, into the opinions of voters with impersonal, expert knowledge, the state university is becoming a part of the citizen's own mind, just

as the state is becoming a part of his will. And that's what the whole story means: the University of Wisconsin is a highly conscious lobe of the common community mind of the people of Wisconsin.

The accomplishment under Van Hise encouraged George E. Vincent, who became president of Minnesota in 1911, to push extension with the zeal that might be expected of the son of the founder of the Chautauqua movement. Vincent invented and developed novel techniques giving his northern university state-wide scope. One of them, born of his knowledge of Chautauqua showmanship, was the "University Week": the visit of a faculty troupe — the word seems appropriate — to some corner of the state to make a circuit of a cluster of towns. They would offer a play on one night, a lecture on the second, a concert on the third, a debate on the fourth, and so on. Out of this superior vaudeville Minnesota in time evolved a remarkably impressive department of concerts and lectures, and an active community program service. Van Hise's labors equally encouraged the University of Indiana, which formally established an extension division in 1912. At a later date Indiana, with nine well-planted extension centers stretching from Gary in the north to Evansville in the south, in effect almost subsidiary colleges, could assert that it possessed one of the most efficient extension programs in the nation.

But breadth of service to democracy was not enough; height was yet more important. Dr. Johnson said of the Scottish, "Their learning is like bread in a besieged town; every man gets a little, but no man gets a full meal." To deserve the title of universities, the state institutions had to think of providing the full meal, satisfying the utmost intellectual and spiritual need, and aiming beyond excellence at distinction. How, in Berkeley and Chapel Hill, in Laramie and Baton Rouge, was this to be done? Andrew D. White, whose mind was enriched by Carlyle, Emerson, and Ruskin, had found a way at Cornell by assembling a galaxy of great teachers, and pouring into the university his own spirit — the spirit expressed in two vital books, his *Autobiography* and his *Warfare of Theology and Science.* How could other universities emulate him?

V

One obvious way was by adding that additional story to university work which Johns Hopkins had first given our higher education. Dr. Angell of Michigan came out vigorously for graduate schools in 1896, asserting that unless the state universities made generous provision for advanced research and teaching they would drift hopelessly behind the endowed seats. "Are the States willing to furnish the means for providing this kind of instruction?" asked Angell. If not, then their universities would be arrested at a low level while endowed institutions pressed upward. Michigan by 1909 had 258 graduate students, and next year organized a separate school. This, it will be remembered, was the year of Princeton's bitter controversy over the site of its new graduate college. Wisconsin in that year also had about 250 graduate students, half in the humanities and half in the sciences. In his inaugural address Van Hise had said: "If the University of Wisconsin is to do for the State what it has a right to expect, it must develop, expand, strengthen creative work at whatever cost." Though his emphasis on research alarmed the regents, it gave comfort to students and faculty. Such scholars as Charles H. Haskins and Frederick Jackson Turner in history, E. A. Ross in sociology, Richard T. Ely in economics, and Grant Showerman in Latin, were attracting ambitious young men and women; so that in 1910 we find Wisconsin conferring 110 master's degrees and eighteen doctorates.

Elsewhere a beginning — a commitment — was made. Down to World War I the principal inferiority of the state universities clearly lay in graduate work. Columbia then led the country in the grant of advanced degrees, with Harvard and Chicago close rivals, while the public universities stood in the rear. Nevertheless, Illinois committed itself in 1905 when James, a man of lofty intellectual standards, organized a separate college of which David Kinley was appointed dean.[16] That same year Minnesota also founded a graduate school. The regents sanctioned it only on an understanding that it would cost nothing and that its head would do as little as possible, but it too was a commitment, and it was soon graduating doctors in science and the humanities. A formally constituted graduate school appeared at Missouri in 1910, and though for a time it catered largely to high school teachers, it again was a commitment. California, which had always given weight to graduate courses, by 1910 had more than 400 graduate students. In these initial undertakings men could read an augury of the day when the state and land-grant institutions would confer far more than half the advanced degrees of the nation.

And in one area research sprang early in the century to a level of very high distinction indeed: in agriculture. The agricultural experiment stations, some antedating the Hatch

[16] David Kinley describes his work for the graduate school in his *Autobiography* (1949), 49-51, 102, but the book is much fuller on his relations with the governor and the legislature. It is unfortunate that few high officers of state universities and land-grant colleges have written their recollections, and these few tend to the dryness of the short books by James B. Angell, John Bascom, and Kinley.

Act and some founded by it, quickly became a group of the most effective agencies of scientific inquiry on the globe. The men who headed these stations looked to Hilgard of California and Burrill of Illinois as pioneers. As early as 1895 Hilgard, with an appropriation of $250, had opened his California laboratory for soil testing and begun experiments on the effect of deep and shallow plowing. He got a little more money later, and the national government employed him to make a thorough study of cotton culture in the United States. While Hilgard was not the first to make a chemical analysis of western soils, he was the first to interpret the results of analyses in relation to plant life and productiveness. He was also the first to point out the loss which the cotton grower sustained by putting cottonseed on his land as fertilizer without first having the valuable oil expressed. Burrill's investigations of the bacterial diseases of plants were famous. The Hatch Act not only multiplied the number of research stations and brought the roster of their scientific workers within a decade to 628; it also improved the character of agricultural instruction, for men who spent part of their time experimenting made abler and fresher teachers. It also lifted research from local and immediate tasks to great fundamental problems — that is, from applied science to pure science.

Research in the humanities could not easily be channeled into extension work. A monograph on Chaucer's imagery did not lend itself to popular dissemination. Far different, however, was the position of agricultural and engineering research — for engineering, too, soon had its experiment stations, the first being organized at Illinois in 1903. The practical results were easily brought home to the bosoms of the people, for they paid in dollars and cents. Experiment stations were soon publishing bulletins, sending out lecturers, reaching into schools, and adopting ever bolder expedients to meet popular needs. Iowa State early in the century sent out "Seed Corn Gospel Trains" with charts, pictures, lecturers, and demonstration materials, a venture so successful that other states imitated it, and in 1911 seventy-one trains reached nearly a million people. The government was meanwhile making its own effort to reach the farmers with "demonstration work"; in the South Rockefeller's General Education Board was assisting; and ere long the most massive machinery in history for bringing the fruits of scientific inquiry directly to the people was in continuous operation.

While graduate work, experiment centers, and research lent increasing distinction to the public universities and colleges, it was their eminent scholars, writers, and teachers who did most to illumine them. As Gilman had said in his Berkeley inaugural in 1872, they were the truest builders. "It is not the site, nor the apparatus, nor the halls, nor the library, nor the board of regents, which draws the students," said Gilman, "it is the body of living teachers, skilled in their specialties, eminent in their callings. . . . Agassiz wherever he goes is surrounded by a company of disciples. Whitney would have his class in language in Berlin or Benares." By the time of World War I the state and land-grant institutions had many teachers of greater eminence than Alexander Agassiz or W. D. Whitney. No person who registered to study American thought with Vernon L. Parrington, or the ballad with Louise Pound, or poetry with William Ellery Leonard, or law with T. M. Cooley, or history with Evarts B. Greene, or psychology with Joseph Jastrow, or criticism with O. W. Firkins, or horticulture with Liberty Hyde Bailey, ever rued his choice. These teachers created a *genius loci,* and their memory hallows the halls in which they taught.

VI

One of the more difficult obligations of these new institutions has been the creation of an atmosphere, a tradition, a sense of the past, which might play as important a part in the education of sensitive students as any other influence. This requires time, sustained attention to cultural values, and the special beauties of landscape or architecture. Nevertheless, sheer affection, the memory of inspiring personalities, and association with important regional events can do a great deal. It is the immemorial grace of towers and lawns, the recollection of great ideas and causes, the fame of eminent leaders, that makes the name Oxford fall like a chime of music on the ears of men in Delhi and Melbourne. It is this which for generations has made men wake at night with memories of Old Nassau at Princeton or the Colonnade in Charlottesville, their warm brick, their ivy, their atmosphere redolent with scholarship and principle. Grim Daniel Webster, telling the Supreme Court, "It is but a small college, yet there are those who love it," wiped his eyes with a surge of affection for the old halls in Hanover. This spiritual grace the state universities cannot quickly acquire, but they have been gaining it.

Filial affection has long since been kindled. Once when a critical appropriation for the University of Minnesota was pending in the legislature, a young champion of the bill learned that the redoubtable Ignatius Donnelly, a fighter for economy, was about to take the floor against it. He went to the Populist leader. "I cannot match your eloquence, Mr.

Donnelly," he pleaded, "So please, if you feel you have to speak, don't speak as effectively as you can." Donnelly made what his friends thought the weakest speech of his career. A graduate of the University of Missouri, recalling the enthusiasm, comradeship, and sense of high purpose which pervaded President Jesse's administration, quotes Wordsworth: "Bliss was it in that dawn to be alive." The University of Alabama, John Craig Stewart tells us, has in special degree an eloquent blending of past and present, a mingling of ghostly memories with the bold progressive present. "Every student sensitive to the tradition of a civilization visible in old buildings, old trees, and faded bronze plaques is conscious of this strange lingering pressure." Here flows the Black Warrior River amid Civil War sites; here is the Gorgas mansion, home of the ordnance chief of the Confederate army, and of his son who helped conquer yellow fever in the Canal Zone; here is the mansion of Alabama governors of a century and more ago; and here are mementos of Jackson and the Creeks. What son of Iowa State does not sometimes hear in fancy the Stanley chimes ringing across the hills? What son of California does not sometimes see the Greek theater rise in a vision before him?

Such a sentiment, once aroused, has the double strength of affection for the university and attachment to the state. One Illinoisian can bear testimony to the birth, in this period, of just these loyalties in the breasts of himself and his youthful comrades. Our university, measured from its rebirth under Draper, was very young. We nevertheless felt that in exuberant vigor, promise for the future, and democracy of spirit, it gave the student a noble stimulus. We knew that its library was not that of Yale or Columbia, but we also knew that it was growing with a rapidity which would soon bring it abreast of these elder collections. We knew that to read the Elizabethan poets under the benign guidance of Stuart P. Sherman was not esteemed by some equal to the privilege of reading them under the harsh glare of George Lyman Kittredge; but we were sure we had the better fortune. We were aware that the old endowed universities had a prestige that gave their degrees better market value than ours; but we also took pride in the fact that students came from New York to study ceramics, that Alvord's volumes on the Mississippi Valley in British politics had opened a field untouched in England, and that P. L. Windsor in the library school, G. T. Flom in Scandinavian studies, and W. S. Robertson in Latin-American history, were unexcelled elsewhere.

We had a feeling, too, that the spirit of the state university was in vital respects richer than the spirit of the endowed institutions. It had a *mystique* all its own, more nourishing than that of schools less closely related to the land. The university had been made by our grandparents and parents, our neighbors, and the men we sent to the legislature; it was by us and of us. From the valleys of Rock River on the north and the Wabash on the east, from the Sangamon, the Kankakee, and the Illinois the best impulses of the state united here — the brightest ambitions, the most determined plans. Coming down from Chicago on the Illinois Central that Douglas had helped endow, through towns where Lincoln had ridden circuit, we saw the towers of the university rise above the undulating prairie with a sense that they were castles of hope and fortresses of the spirit. We knew how deeply the university's roots penetrated into every locality of the state. One lad who had driven six miles to listen to Cyril G. Hopkins speak on soil fertility, who had watched the university inspector walk into his country high school and buttonhole the principal, who had heard Clarence W. Alvord speak to a meeting of teachers, and who knew what an original impulse Chauncey Baldwin had given the study of the Bible from Lake Forest to Cairo — that lad deemed the university a familiar friend before he entered his first classroom at eight o'clock on a bright autumn morning, and caught the first glinting ideas from the brilliant mind of Jacob Zeitlin.

VII

H. G. Wells, in his fascinating apologue "The Food of the Gods," pictures the mingling of good and bad consequences in unrestrained growth. The urchin who grows to giant size could perform a giant's tasks, but his misstep smashed the drains. The giant flower was wondrously beautiful, but its fragrance was coarsened. By 1910 the land-grant colleges and state universities were beginning to eat of the food of the gods; they had proved themselves so worthy of popular support that this support was swelling their size. David Kinley in his memoirs tells how, at the request of President James, he once went to Chicago to ask the aid of a powerful friend of the university in saving a threatened appropriation. The friend dispatched two sets of telegrams to different groups in the legislature; one was a peremptory order, the other a polite request; and the appropriation passed. In 1910 the total attendance at Cornell and Michigan well exceeded 5,000, and Illinois, Wisconsin, and Minnesota almost touched that figure. The entire land-grant enrollment in 1910, according to E. D. Eddy, was 73,536. At this time the sixteen universities of France had an enrollment of 40,001 matriculated students, and all the German universities, after a spectacular increase, 54,845 students.

The flood tide was just setting in. Dr. Slosson, writing of the "unprecedented growth," which far outstripped the rise in population, states that when he asked the cause, men told him at one university, "That was when we got a new president"; at another, "That was the year of the big corn crop"; at a third, "The new school law came into effect just then." Actually, the curve of growth was the same all over the country; some universal law was at work. High schools had been stimulated by the expansion of university opportunity, and they in turn stimulated higher education. Professions were multiplying, and the public universities, intent on maintaining an open society, threw wide the avenues leading to them. Agriculture was now more than a profession — it was one of the busiest and most fruitful areas of experimental science known to research. Dean Davenport could report in 1912 the complete justification of Jonathan B. Turner, writing: "most of the better agricultural colleges are overflowing with students, and many of them are discussing the best methods of limiting attendance." Public appreciation meant not only a quickened flow of appropriations, but also an energetic defense against all enemies.

And while the older land-grant institutions grew, new institutions were coming to birth. In the last twenty years of the century eight new agricultural and engineering colleges appeared, from Clemson in South Carolina to New Mexico; eleven Negro land-grant institutions, from South Carolina to Oklahoma;[17] and five new state universities,

[17] The rise of really vigorous Negro land-grant colleges dated from the requirement in the second Morrill Act that federal endowments be fairly divided between Negroes and whites, with explicit reports to the government.

including Arizona, Wyoming, and Idaho. Growth, or rather the extraordinary rapidity of growth, posed formidable new problems. But one issue had been settled. Educators no longer debated the question whether they should train the elite, or the masses; they saw that they did not need to make a choice — if they planned well, they could train both.

(IV)

POISED FOR

A NEW CENTURY

ONE HUNDRED years after the Morrill Act which founded them, the land-grant colleges and universities faced the same central problem as they did at the outset: how could they best be of service to democracy? They had decisively won some of the battles which such early leaders as Ezra Cornell, Jonathan B. Turner, and Justin S. Morrill expected them to fight. Long since, they had helped deliver a deathblow to the narrow program of classical studies which bestrode so much of higher education in 1860. Long since, too, they had lifted agriculture from the status of a manual calling to that of a profession, had raised the "mechanic arts" from mere trades to the dignity of a series of expert professional callings, and both in academic training and research had given agriculture and engineering a scientific character of high standing. Meanwhile, they had done much to make coeducation a standard feature of American academic life, and to divorce university work from religious trammels. By severe struggles, often in hostile environments, the greater land-grant institutions had preserved and improved the essential disciplines in pure science and the humanities.

The central battle, however, is never fully won. As in 1870 and 1900, the most vital task of these institutions remained the fortification and enrichment of democracy. It had to be reexamined in the light of the sweeping changes of the period; the emergence of the welfare state, the increased affluence of society, the cold war, the demand for large-scale scientific instruction, and above all, newer ideals of general education. At the time Ezra Cornell said he wished to found a university in which any student could pursue any study to the height of his ability, even a good high school education was attained by few. By 1960 it was within the grasp of nearly all, and the time was at hand when a college education would be taken nearly as much for granted as secondary training. The colleges and universities had to serve democracy by molding unprecedented numbers.

The essential character of this training remained much what it had always been. Our perdurable democratic ideals are freedom and equality. Coping with numbers, the state and land-grant universities have an ever more difficult responsibility for promoting freedom in inquiry, freedom in the discussion of ideas, and freedom in the dissemination of truth, however unpopular. They must deal with cross sections of the whole population, and the worst tyranny is often mass tyranny. Numbers unquestionably complicate the task of keeping our nation an open and a mobile society. Higher education has a prime function in contributing to equality of opportunity by giving every ambitious person, young or old, rich or poor, well trained or ill trained, a chance adapted to his or her gifts. But the avenues of opportunity may become choked, and in training millions of students — perhaps soon ten millions — it will not be as easy as it was to foster a healthy diversity in intellectual and social life, to encourage social experimentation, and to nurture tolerance and liberalism.

In accepting their democratic responsibilities, the public universities and colleges enjoy three relatively new advantages. The first is that, as President David D. Henry of the University of Illinois writes, they now move from a position of strength. Two overlapping groups, about seventy land-grant institutions out of ninety-four major state-supported seats of learning, constitute the most impressive set of agencies for higher education in the world. They stretch from Puerto Rico to Hawaii. They enroll about one-third of the college and university students of the nation. Their graduate schools have trained more than half of the country's holders of doctoral degrees. They include the largest of our universities, and their sisters among endowed institutions agree that their financial resources will ultimately be unmatchable. In the light of these facts, public confidence and support steadily grow. When the University of Michigan was denied aid in its early days of struggle, President Tappan told the legislature: "Very well, gentlemen; but when my students sit in your places, the story will be different." In Michigan and most other states the graduates now sit in the capitals and write a very different story.

The second great advantage is that the high schools of the land, or at any rate of the more populous states, are enjoying an encouraging renascence. Responding to a barrage of public criticism, to insistent comparisons with foreign secondary schools, and to the stimulation of such men as President James B. Conant, they show a real if uneven elevation in efficiency and standards. The quality of the high schools largely determines the quality of undergraduate work in the public universities. Their improvement gives hope that we may yet see them equal the best British, French, and German secondary schools.

In the enrichment of democracy, meanwhile, the public universities have as a third advantage the continued plasticity of higher education in the United States. They began as experiments a century ago, and experimentation shows no pause in velocity. Many men are advocating an acceleration of university work which will give registrants the bachelor's degree in three years and the master's in four. The best high schools are striving to take over much of college freshman work, and to gain their brighter students advanced placement. The small colleges, largely under pressures from the state universities, have begun forming confederations to give their training greater efficiency: the Midwestern group led by Knox, Beloit, and Carleton, the Great Lakes group, the Virginia constellation, and others. A new type of university president is emerging, as different from Andrew D. White or Charles R. Van Hise as White was different from Eliphalet Nott. Novel methods in higher education are teaching us strange phrases like "program learning," and are wresting teachers out of old ruts. Television is made a magical new aid by lecturers such as the poet John G. Neihardt at the University of Missouri.

To a foreign visitor inquiring about land-grant colleges we might show the University of California as an archetype of versatile growth in the fast-changing scene and as an augury of the great state institutions to come. This university in 1961 had nine seats: two fully equipped campuses in Berkeley and Los Angeles, four more vigorously planted in Davis, San Francisco, Santa Barbara, and Riverside, and three coming into existence in San Diego, Orange County, and on the south-central coast. The university enrolled in 1961 nearly 45,000 students, it had by then granted a total of about 300,000 degrees, and it had a quarter of a million living graduates. Of the world's Nobel Prize winners, eight took their degrees there, and eight or nine were on the staff. The Association of American Colleges had pronounced the graduate program the second strongest in the country, and the university extension program was the largest in the world. Yet the institution had attained leviathan stature only since its real growth began about 1890. In size and vigor some of the Midwestern universities pressed close behind it.[1]

I

Observers of higher education can now foresee the inexorable emergence of an entirely new landscape. It will no longer show us a nation dotted by high academic peaks with lesser hills between; it will be a landscape dominated by mountain ranges. California's nine university campuses will constitute an especially massive range. Of the nine, four are being planned or replanned to hold 27,500 students each, three to hold 15,000 apiece, and the other two 17,500 between them, each with an appropriate faculty, library, laboratories, and full graduate equipment. These nine university campuses are flanked by sixteen state colleges, under a single coordinating head; each college with an actual or potential five-year course of study.

New York is planning an even more massive range, for a committee on higher education under Henry T. Heald has

[1] See "Year of Decision for California Higher Education," University of California (1960); University of California, *Report of the President for the Academic Year 1960-61, Incorporating the Summary Report of Operations* (1961).

just reported that by 1985 the number of New Yorkers wishing to do college work either full time or part time can be expected to reach 1,270,000, more than half of whom will have to turn to public institutions. Michigan, with large state-supported universities in Ann Arbor, East Lansing, and Detroit, a college at Flint, and a university center in Dearborn, has another solid range taking shape. Illinois has its own range, from Chicago to Carbondale, in process of creation. Minnesota has three state university campuses in the three principal centers of population, and Wisconsin has been astonished by the swift rise of its new university branch in Milwaukee.

Against this landscape of emergent mountain ranges, the endowed institutions, from Harvard to Stanford, still lift their separate peaks. The characteristics which distinguish them from state-supported universities are being blurred, to be sure, by two fairly novel tendencies.

For one, much of their nutriment is drawn today from public funds. Columbia, Yale, Duke, Chicago, and others would be hard hit, and several would stagger, if their large federal incomes, direct and indirect, were withdrawn; and Columbia, for one, has served its own state government almost as closely as the University of Wisconsin ever did. On the other side of the line, the state universities and land-grant institutions increasingly profit from private benefactions. The University of California in Berkeley has been privately endowed with its matchless site, its Lick observatory, its Bancroft Library, and the gifts of Phoebe Hearst and others. The thousand-acre campus of its new Orange County branch is a gift from the fabulous Irvine Ranch. Indeed, in the academic year 1958-59 the University of California obtained well over ten millions from private sources. That year saw the consolidated endowment fund of the University of Michigan go above thirteen millions; while quite apart from endowment, it had earlier received from the Ford Motor Company the largest single gift in its history. This was the Fair Lane residence of Henry Ford, with 210 acres and $6,500,000 for establishing a two-year senior college with its own library, laboratories, and faculty in one of the busiest industrial centers of the nation. Corporations and foundations, in fact, now make as liberal grants to state universities as to endowed institutions.

Thus from two sides the line between public and endowed seats of higher education is being somewhat blurred. A vital difference nevertheless remains, and it is of the highest importance that it should never disappear. Historically, the endowed universities have given a superior leadership in many fields, largely because they have had a greater freedom of action; and in some fields they can continue to do so. A certain division of labor in university training is an old and valuable feature of our cultural life. The two sets of institutions, partners rather than rivals, will always have much to contribute to each other in ideas and spirit.

The national landscape as a whole still had in 1962 its flatly disappointing areas and its regions where the struggle remained hard. In some of the Rocky Mountain states the universities were still subject to political interference and unfair pressures from powerful economic interests. Various land-grant colleges remained shockingly weak in the humanities. Kansas State College did not grant its first bachelor of arts degree until 1959. The University of Alabama, for all its fine traditions, was not able to award the doctorate in biology, chemistry, or history until 1950. It is refreshing to find President Logan Wilson of the University of Texas writing in his report for 1956-57 that his institution had no illusions; it knew it was not yet distinguished, though it was "definitely on the way to becoming a university truly of the first class" — a statement more modest than we usually get from Texas. Political interferences with the work done at Austin are well within memory. The University of New Hampshire has lately made tactful complaint, which some of its land-grant neighbors in New England might echo, of Yankee stinginess; it has a millage formula of tax support, but a problem in getting it consistently met.

And most distressing of all, standards of admission in the weakest state universities remain deplorable. Any high school graduate with a *C* average can get in, especially if he does well in a college aptitude test. Some large and strong universities, meanwhile, find half the students who enter dropping out — or pushed out — along the way; a fact which, after all discounts, points to an appalling waste of students' and teachers' time.

Observers who find the gargantuan statistics of present and prospective enrollment disconcerting will nevertheless commit a flagrant error if they suppose that great size is in itself reprehensible. The error has a simply psychological root. A total of 30,000 students seems alarming to the man who relates it to the kind of university he attended with 6,000 students. Of course attendances of 30,000 are not related to that kind of institution at all. The crucial question, as President Henry of Illinois says, is not size but rate of increase. In the larger, wealthier states most planners agree that once a university is well established an average growth of 10 per cent a year presents no alarming problems. In some departments that level may be too high, and in some, too low, but it is generally practicable. A new institution, of course, requires a slower pace of expansion. The Milwaukee branch of the University of Wisconsin has to move more deliberately than the Madison half, and the Santa Barbara campus of the University of California more cautiously than the Berkeley campus. When enrollment in Milwaukee went up by 9.6 per cent in one year, laboratories and other elements were seriously overstrained.

Size and rate of growth hoist danger signals only when they become disproportionate to existing facilities and faculty, to financial resources, and above all, to administrative capacity. As with lower schools, time factors are important. The experienced heads of the University of California tell us: "It requires a considerable effort — almost a crash program — to get started at all, and to add the second thousand of students to a campus of one thousand is more difficult than to add the eleventh thousand to a campus of ten thousand." In short, growth must be controlled by a time-size-resources equation if the state is not to endanger academic standards. California has learned that "to bring a new campus to the point where it can enroll 7,500 students will require a total 'lead-time' of about fifteen years." Thereafter, a campus with 10,000 to 20,000 students can safely grow by 1,500 a year, and a campus with 20,000 or 25,000 students may even grow annually by 2,250 students. To be sure, California's resources are huge, and as Daniel Coit Gilman said nearly a century ago, it has a "passion" for education.

The sharpest strain in growth lies not in finding able teachers, but expert administrators. The new type of president required by the mountain-range universities will be a coordinator rather than a creative leader. He must help the various campuses or branches to work harmoniously; he must deal skillfully with legislators, regents, faculty, students, and the public. He holds a place more closely resembling the corporation executive than the old type of inspirational college president. Not that inspiration is unimportant, for the difference between an exalted and a commonplace university has sometimes depended on the amount of light and warmth radiated by the head. If he has the brilliance of a William Rainey Harper, he may accomplish wonders. But in the university systems it is more important that he be an expert executive, a tactful moderator, and a good public relations man; more important that he be able to place his finger on capable deans and other lieutenants. President Robert Gordon Sproul, of California, was such an executive, adapted to the giant university, who moved into his post not from an academic station but from the comptrollership. Though nobody ever doubted his success, he seemed a world away not only from Eliot and Butler, but also from Van Hise and E. J. James. He made effective use, in talking to legislators, of Stanford. Are you content, he said in effect, that the rich man's child should find a distinguished institution at Stanford or some Eastern seat, while your parsimony keeps the child of the plain citizen in an inferior university? He had the wisdom to offer high salaries to attract a group of distinguished professors. Their preference in pay excited a little jealous heartburn, but the mere fact of their residence made it easier to attract other superior scholars. Able teachers went to Berkeley to be near Herbert E. Bolton in history, or George Rapall Noyes in Slavic studies, or the Nobel Prize winners in science. Still more important was the fact that as the university became colossal and its parts sprawled all over our third largest state, Sproul kept it in cohesion and maintained the balance of its parts. He well knew how to find able subordinate executives.

In this task of coordinating and harmonizing a university of huge size, the trustees or regents are more important than ever before. The importance of an alert, liberal-minded, hard-working board cannot be overestimated. It should be a board which, if not completely free from interference by the state government, like that of Michigan, is at any rate open only to strictly limited pressures. One keen observer of academic affairs, Mr. Paul H. Davis, formerly of Stanford and Columbia, asserts that the most infallible sign of a decaying college is a set of lazy, passive, conservative trustees, and one of the certain signs of a progressive, vigorous institution is a board of wide-awake, earnest, far-sighted men. He ranks the boards he has observed in four main groups. At the top stand the trustees of the older endowed institutions, such as Harvard, Yale, Princeton, and Columbia. Next, with great unevenness, come the state universities, the appointive boards being better than the elective. A step lower down, of course with notable exceptions, he finds the boards of small endowed colleges. Finally, at the bottom are the boards of the religiously affiliated colleges, stained not only by incompetency, but by some outright dishonesty. It is in the church school that he most frequently meets the trustee with an eye on a contract for his business firm.

That the state university boards should hold second rank is unfortunate. This is probably one of the inevitable consequences of their democratic origin and character. When the people elect trustees, they may now and then think the fame of a football star sufficient passport to partial control of their university; and under any system a Dave Beck may creep in, or such a myopic conservative as the corporation attorney who seriously damaged Berkeley by insistence on a loyalty oath. But as higher education becomes a gigantic machine, involving hundreds of millions and the most sensitive interests of the whole people, carefully chosen boards become a necessity.

In growth, the primary problems in providing libraries, laboratories, gifted teachers, and residential halls are plain enough. Much more complex are the before-noted problems of balance. Professional schools, scientific schools, technological schools, and liberal arts schools should be kept in Newtonian correspondence with each other and with public demand. Some balance must be maintained between undergraduate and graduate work, between instruction and research. Above all, balance should be achieved between the great idea of education for doing, so dear to the professional schools in land-grant institutions, and the still greater ideal of education for being, so stubbornly cherished by all true humanists and many scientists.

The value of balance, to be sure, can be exaggerated, and it is sometimes best thrown out of the window. Eccentricity in the distribution of money and effort is commendable in the pursuit of some special excellence, some supreme achievement. Balance and restraint went to the winds when the University of Indiana determined on an annual presentation of Wagner's *Parsifal;* when the University of Arkansas put a million dollars into an art center; when the University of California encouraged E. O. Lawrence to build his cyclotron; when the University of Kentucky and its Press undertook publication of the complete writings of Henry Clay; when the University of Texas paid more than a million dollars at a single sale of books and manuscripts in London to swell its treasures in English literature; when the University of Alabama formed its chamber music organization to play all over the state; and when the University of Michigan launched a $7,600,000 project for research in the peaceful uses of atomic energy, dedicated to the memory of the university's dead in World War II — a project which at once received $1,000,000 from the Ford Motor Company for a nuclear reactor.

Distinction, at the cost of a certain imbalance, is best embodied in the graduate schools of the state universities; for from them pour out, year by year, the future leaders of the states in science, engineering, law, business, and the humanities — in everything except some creative arts. It is in the graduate schools that research makes its greatest contributions to human welfare. In the greater state universities, graduate enrollments are rising at a substantially higher rate than undergraduate registration, and this tendency seems certain to continue. As society grows more complex, as knowledge advances, and as international competition becomes fiercer, the need for very highly trained men and women in a great variety of fields becomes more exigent.

"It comes as a shock to many people," President Harlan Hatcher of the University of Michigan wrote in 1959, "to realize that 38 per cent of the students on our campus are now graduates or graduate professionals who already have a baccalaureate degree. The programs, laboratories and libraries, faculties, and facilities required for this operation are quite different from the needs of the typical undergraduate college." Michigan's enrollment in her Horace H. Rackham School of Graduate Studies in 1958 in fact exceeded 5,400, and that spring she awarded 1,900 advanced degrees. The Rockefeller brothers' report lays strong emphasis on the fact that the ratio to undergraduates must keep on rising. California in 1955 awarded 1,415 advanced degrees and four years later fell just short of 2,000. Sixty departments in the University of Wisconsin now give the doctorate of philosophy, and in 1959 they granted about 350 such doctorates. The story in the other major state universities — Illinois, Minnesota, Indiana, Missouri, Ohio State, Texas — is much the same. Numbers would be still larger if some of these universities did not severely limit admission from outside their respective states.

Research is the central occupation of all graduate schools, and certain achievements of research teachers have been spectacular. It was no small feat for Professor James A. Van Allen at the University of Iowa to penetrate the significance of the two so-called Van Allen zones of intense radiation which encircle the earth; no small feat for Professor B. H. Hopkins and his assistants at the University of Illinois to discover, as they thought, the element illinium, or for Dr. Joseph T. Tykociner there to develop his combination of sight and sound on film; no small feat for University of Wisconsin experts to find a means of irradiating food to lift its vitamin-D content, or for workers in the University Speech Clinic in Ann Arbor to elaborate new medical, social, and psychological treatments of defective articulation. Ohio State has a bureau of business research which not only collects and distributes current information but also makes exhaustive studies of problems affecting a whole industry and publishes the results in its *Bulletin of Business Research.*

Perhaps the University of Minnesota bears off the prize for the most remarkable practical benefit yet conferred on a state by engineering research. Minnesota early established an experiment station in its school of mines, and by 1922 it had developed sufficient power to deal with the most menacing industrial situation the region had yet known. Just after World War I the state faced the alarming prospect of losing its iron industry, for the best ores of the Mesabi range, soft, rich, and easily scooped, were being exhausted. The remaining minerals of the Mesabi and Cuyuna ranges were so refractory that experts doubted whether machinery and methods could ever be devised to work them. To an analysis of this taconite rock, approximately one-third good ore and the remainder waste, Edward W. Davis and other university men devoted years of study. By hard toil they mastered difficulty after difficulty until they finally made the enormous deposits of taconite, sufficient to supply the nation with steel for generations, completely available; a memorable service not only to Proctor Knott's zenith state of the unsalted seas, but also to the whole country.

The variety of research services offered by the state universities is, indeed, astonishing. Indiana has not only her center of English studies in the marvelous Lilly Library, but a valuable and original research enterprise in anthropology, folklore, and linguistics. Its activities in one recent year ranged from interviews with metropolitan leaders of Greek, Mexican, Yugoslav, and other national-origin groups to "a collection of lascivious limericks (gathered locally)." The Indiana University Press has paid especial regard to books on folklore. Illinois furnishes advanced students the resources of the H. G. Wells archive, the Horner collection on Lincoln, and the Hollander collection in economics, while its important research publications range from parasitology to John Milton.

The founding of the Kentucky Life Museum by the University of Kentucky, which is filling an old Greek Revival mansion and its slave quarters with antique furniture, tools, instruments, costumes, pictures, and other relics is an appealing innovation.

If we fancy a defensive note in the statements of the University of Minnesota on its department of mortuary science, certainly no such chord is struck in Michigan State's account of its studies in Midwestern culture. Minnesota may well take pride in the work of its Hormel Institute (founded by the head of a well-known commercial firm) upon better ways of using plant and animal food. How warmly Henry David Thoreau and John Muir, not to mention Charles R. Van Hise, would have welcomed Michigan's school of natural resources, which not only encourages conservation of forests, soil, and waterpower, but also conducts original studies in watershed management, forest fire control, and wildlife diseases. It is good to learn that while one Michigan professor studies Washington Irving's relations with Germany and another the philosophy of value, while one group toils at the control of arthritis and a second prosecutes the publication of a Middle English dictionary, a dedicated scientist devotes ten years to a study of the aging deer of Southern Michigan. The motto of the state universities is taken from Samuel Rogers: "Think nothing done while aught remains to do."

Yet in the research field it is the agricultural experiment stations which have given our economy and hence our life the most distinctively American and most broadly effective accretions. The 4,000 scientists who were working in them at the time of Pearl Harbor, and the much larger number they employ today, have poured out a steady stream of discoveries and innovations; and the extension apparatus provided by the Smith-Lever Act, the Bankhead-Jones Act, and other federal laws has carried the results with magnificent speed and effectiveness to the farm population. The stations have united with each other and with the federal Department of Agriculture in cooperative research; they have published bulletins by the hundred thousands; they have used county farm bureaus, the 4-H clubs, the granges, and other groups in applying their findings. They have been quick to utilize such recent aids as the radioactive isotopes. Two generations after the primitive day when Isaac Roberts at Cornell dug up some dead horses and placed his class "on the windward side" to study anatomy, Admiral Lewis L. Strauss declared publicly that the land-grant colleges were setting "the highest standards of research to be found anywhere." They fully realize that pure science must be pursued as earnestly as applied science.

To the experiment stations goes the principal credit for the astonishing rise of the soybean industry. They may claim most of the honor for the development of hybrid corn, which has supposedly increased crop yields by nearly one-third. They have originated important new varieties of apples, pears, cherries, and other fruits, and have improved the breeds of wheat, oats, and other grains. From them have sprung better methods of controlling insect pests and plant diseases. The labors of Jacob G. Lipman and Selden A. Waksman at the New Jersey experiment station upon soil micro-organisms culminated in the discovery of streptomycin. It is largely because of this unrivaled partnership of research and practical extension work that 8 per cent of the American population have been able to produce food for the whole nation, and that farm leaders expect to see eventually 4 per cent accomplishing the task. Those who have never watched the boys and girls of a 4-H club at work have missed one of the best existing exemplifications of democracy. Engineering experiment stations, meanwhile, have followed in the path of agriculture.

But however important the post-graduate departments of the public universities, their research undertakings, and the extension programs that make all the state a campus, their central responsibility to democracy still lies in undergraduate instruction. The most perplexing problem they face in dealing with rapid and irresistible growth is the selection of their students; the problem of providing a fair opportunity to all aspiring and worthy young people when the high schools turn out an almost unmanageable flood of them. President Edwin B. Fred of the University of Wisconsin recently said: "Maintenance of quality will be difficult in the years immediately ahead. We shall have serious space restrictions. We shall have to develop new methods for handling the growing numbers of students. No part of this is easy."

That view is almost universally shared. Wisconsin by 1970 is expected to have 350,000 young people of college age, and every state from North Dakota to Florida will present comparable numbers. How can the universities encourage and nurture the best without discouraging the second best? — for heads of all the state institutions feel that they have a democratic duty. They have to echo Dean Charles W. Sanford of the University of Illinois: "The university is trying to help students at *all* levels of ability." They have to take the view of the heads of the University of California, who have just declared: "Opportunity for higher education in California will continue to be available for *all* qualified students."

One means of lessening the magnitude of the problem is

seldom discussed and should be approached with caution, but has real validity. It is to diffuse a more thoughtful attitude toward college attendance. Too many young people embark upon higher education because it is the correct social move, expected by family and friends, and leading automatically to the higher status described by Vance Packard. No such attitude existed in the America of 1890, and no such attitude prevails in Britain, France, or Scandinavia today. Purely automatic college attendance is a misfortune to everybody: to the better-motivated students, the faculty, and the taxpayer. If a century ago we made much too little of college, today we make rather too much. Discouragement in some instances is important, and certainly a diploma elite is unhealthy. Everybody should realize that Mr. Truman without college could be quite as good a President as Mr. Coolidge with an Amherst degree.

Every close observer of life — not education, but life — learns that bright and worthy young men may lose in exchanging the tough discipline of office, workshop, or competitive enterprise for the looser discipline of classes. Horace Greeley had some reason for preferring journalists trained in the rough school of life, like Samuel Bowles and James Gordon Bennett, to the "horned cattle" of colleges. Probably Mark Twain would have been wilted rather than freshened by college, and he assuredly got more out of steamboating on the Mississippi and knocking about in Nevada and California. We may be well content that Lincoln's sole academic experience was going in one door of Knox and coming out another with the wry remark, "At last I have been through college." Walt Whitman would doubtless have been injured by four college years; they might have made him another Longfellow. The late Abraham Flexner, who knew John D. Rockefeller, Sr., well and greatly admired him, used to say emphatically that Rockefeller would have been retarded, not aided, by a college; his genius for organization, his bold defiance of old patterns, would have been fettered. With hardly less certainty we can say the same of Carnegie, of George Westinghouse (who went to Union for three months), of Cyrus H. McCormick, and indeed of most of the Samuel Smiles clan.

Even a more rational view of diploma values, however, will not substantially diminish our problem. One overriding fact is that the age composition of the country is changing. In 1955 the young Americans between fifteen and twenty-four, according to the Rockefeller brothers' report, numbered 22,000,000, and in 1975 they will number 48,000,000 — more than double! How choose among them, especially in view of the pronounced shortage of highly trained talent? A vast national effort, with special programs on campus after campus, is being made to discover and develop the specially fit.

The predominant mode of selection is as yet simply a choice of the high school elite. The University of California under its new master plan counts on taking only the best eighth of high school graduates. The University of Wisconsin by 1956 took well over half its freshmen from the top quarter of the high school classes, and less than 5 per cent from the bottom quarter; the University of Illinois in 1958 took approximately half from the top quarter, and less than 6 per cent from the bottom quarter. All public universities assert that the quality of the entering students has improved tremendously in the last twenty years. Their own requirements have become stricter; the high schools have grown more efficient; and a larger proportion of the very able young people have decided to enter the state university instead of an endowed institution. Some universities, like Indiana, are assisted in selecting students by an especially close relationship with the high schools, for they send faculty members about to lecture and to consult with prospective entrants, while they invite interested members of the upper half of the graduating classes to spend a day at the university.

But the task of selection, as both endowed and public universities admit, involves endless uncertainties. The fact is that no trustworthy means exists for determining which students are exceptional, which average, and which dull. Selection officers in Columbia and Princeton are as ready as those at Illinois and Minnesota to admit that appalling mistakes are possible, which in totality may amount to a cruel social injustice.

Many young people who do not seem "academically talented" — the phrase of the Carnegie Corporation — may merely be retarded by environment, or by inner repressions. Moreover, talent depends on relationships, and a man dull in one context may be brilliant in another. Oliver Goldsmith was flogged as a dunce and stood at the bottom of his class in Trinity College. James McNeil Whistler was flunked out of West Point; "if silicon had been a gas," he said later, "I would have been a major-general." Another important consideration is that the dullards stand among the parents of the next generation, and from the home of the dullard may come the supremely gifted, as from Thomas Lincoln's cabin came Abraham Lincoln. It will make a difference if the Thomas Lincolns have been given their full chance. Finally, a commitment is a commitment; the state and land-grant institutions are committed to give every youngster opportunities adequate to the best interpretation of his powers. In this hazardous zone the trustees of the Carnegie Corporation, acting with Presidents Pusey of Harvard, Kirk of Columbia, Griswold of Yale, Meredith Wilson of Minnesota, Murphy of UCLA, and Logan Wilson of Texas, have offered a set of cautionary rules. Their first injunction is that the diagnosis of a youngster's abilities should ideally be a process continued over long years, with repeated tests, regular reappraisals by school marks, and fresh annual judgments by teachers and counselors. Even with all this, they say, we may err: "There are enigmas in individual development which we have not fathomed." The second rule is that appraisals should be founded on many kinds of tests. Scholastic aptitude, achievement, and grades are all precarious, and should be measured against each other. In addition, full weight must be given to what modern pedagogues call motivation and our grandfathers called earnestness. The plodding boy who polishes up the big brass knocker with Gilbertian passion will become Secretary of the Navy while the clever snatcher of *A* marks remains a lieutenant j.g., for after all, character counts quite as much as brains.

Once the students are admitted, universities still face the central question — education for what? Two general opinions on this issue stand in sharp opposition. President A. Lawrence Lowell's view was that higher education is worth having and worth giving, for its pervasive effect on the man or woman who received it. Mental discipline is good in itself; the expansion of the imagination is good in itself; the inculcation of an austere set of standards is good in itself. Any study which challenges and braces the mind, any intellectual task which imposes a severe discipline is good in itself even if it leads to no practical end. The opposed view was laid down by J. McKeen Cattell: the only true ideal of higher education is that which measures its results in terms of specific achievement in after life. Most engineers, agriculturists, and businessmen would accept the latter view.

Actually the two ideals are by no means mutually exclusive, and account should be taken of both. Some students best lend themselves to one, and some to the other. It might be supposed that Cattell's more practical theory would be accepted, explicitly or implicitly, in state universities dependent on public funds. For what, the critic of Lowell would exclaim, shall we use money wrung from the taxpayers, money that is a public trust — just for individual betterment, for enriching the soul of one man and improving the aesthetic sensibilities of another? No, public moneys should be devoted to public service, as in training a better farm expert or more efficient electrical engineer. Happily, most heads of state and land-grant institutions have never taken this narrow outlook. They have always understood that any community is stronger for having in its midst a body of cultivated and discriminating men and women, their intellectual interests deepened by liberal studies, even if their cultivation never finds pragmatic outlets. Our best state university presidents today are as intent on education for *being* as on education for *doing*.

Another question connected with student selection is increasingly urgent: shall student aid be given on a basis of need, or a basis of merit? As enrollment and costs increase, more aid, aid on a massive scale, will be required. Fewer than one-fifth of the nation's families, according to recent inquiries, can afford the full cost of college education for all their children, yet nearly two-fifths of the families now send youngsters to college, and the proportion will soon be one-half. A former faculty member declares: "Harvard is rapidly becoming a college serving only upper-middle-income families." Harvard's Dean William J. Bender, who supervises admissions and financial aids, has calculated that by 1970 the annual price tag for a Harvard education will be $4,000 to $5,000, and less than 5 per cent of American families will be able to pay it from their own resources. As the *New York Times* remarks, the whole structure of our higher education "is in an economic log-jam." In public and private universities alike, the program of aids through loans, jobs, or scholarships will have to be enlarged if we are to make proper use of our best resource — human ability.

Most American universities, like Harvard, grant aid primarily on a basis of need — the fundamental scholastic requirements being met, of course. So do the English universities. Harvard has in fact carefully computed the assistance needed by a two-child family, a three-child family, and so on. The Woodrow Wilson National Scholarship Foundation, on the contrary, uses a merit basis. It gives each fellow selected for graduate study a fixed stipend, be his parents rich or poor, and pays his fees at the university of his choice. Supplementary stipends are even granted to cover such additional costs as those entailed by marriage. The payment is a subsidy to excellency and promise, not need. Russia's system is to give the university student, who is chosen primarily for promise, not only a free education but also a salary, just as some of our business enterprises offer paid training programs for novitiates. But our state and land-grant universities have a historic commitment to the education of the poor, and in providing for undergraduates will assuredly continue to make need the more essential qualification.[2]

The fundamental question remains: how shall state universities and land-grant schools reconcile with democracy a more and more rigid sieving out of the majority of high school students? President Henry of Illinois states in his report for 1958-59: "Denials totaled about 2,500 this year, as opposed to about 1,700 in 1957-58. . . ." Bravo! — but where shall the 2,500 go? Where shall the 2,000 who were dropped from Ohio State in a single year go?[3]

The best answer to such questions thus far devised seems to be that offered by California's so-called master plan. In California the nine-branched university will accept only high school graduates of *A* rank; the sixteen state colleges, broadly speaking, will take the *B* students; and the municipal junior colleges, now nearly sixty in number, will take the *C* students, who at the end of two years may have shown qualities entitling them to transfer to the university. The plan is still experimental. It has already yielded one curious

[2] The question of aid to needy students is covered in *College Board Review*, no. 20, May, 1953, and subsequent issues. The *Report of the President of Indiana University* (1957-58) makes a fairly representative statement on student loan service. During that academic year Indiana granted 1,073 short-term and 163 long-term loans, to a total sum of more than $120,000.

[3] Catalogues of 1960 show numerous examples of land-grant institution requirements for admission. The University of Kentucky accepted students who offered fifteen units of high school work, recommendation by the principal, and a suitable score in the university classification test. Special students were admitted without a high school diploma if at least twenty-one years old, and "fully prepared to do the work required." The State University of South Dakota admitted those who offered sixteen units of work from an accredited high school, without stipulation as to grades; accepted students from nonaccredited high schools by special examination; and took unclassified students over twenty-one if they provided evidence of fitness to pursue college work. This list could be much extended.

result: since women make *A* grades more frequently than men, they seem to be gaining a predominance in Berkeley and UCLA. Costs of the whole system, too, are unexpectedly high. Yet the plan is so promising that it has won general acceptance, has been commended to other states by President Conant, and has manifestly affected the proposals just made in the state of New York by its distinguished committee on higher education, Henry T. Heald, Marion B. Folsom, and John W. Gardner — proposals looking toward the day in 1985 when New York will have 635,000 full-time college students, and as many more half-time.[4]

This committee asks that New York also prepare a master plan. It calls for a rapid expansion of the state university system, with graduate programs not only at existing centers of the system, such as Syracuse and Buffalo, but in two new public universities, the equals of Cornell, one on Long Island, and one upstate. It proposes the conversion of the eleven colleges of education in New York into liberal arts colleges, which should continue to train teachers but should train others, up to the master's degree, as well. The committee in this recommendation remarks that "professional courses in education have been increased out of proportion to the legitimate subject matter," and should be cut back. Finally, the committee urges the creation of a numerous flock of two-year community colleges, state aided, but locally supported and administered, with low tuition charges, their doors flung wide to the young people in their areas. Existing two-year colleges should be expanded and

[4] The University of North Carolina has experimented with a "superior freshman program," placing groups of specially gifted freshmen together in classes of mathematics, western civilization, philosophy, and English, and found the results "gratifying." The University of North Carolina, *President's Report,* 1954-55, 1955-56.

new colleges opened, with sufficient celerity to provide for 125,000 full-time students within less than two decades.

This plan, obviously, parallels that of California: a number of great universities at the top, providing broad undergraduate and professional instruction as well as graduate work; a body of four- or five-year colleges beside them, including the four New York City colleges; and scattered over the state an array of community or junior colleges easily reached by the poorest families, and ready to make as much as possible out of even *C* students. The committee boldly suggested that a tuition rebate of $300 a year be given automatically to all *C* average or better students from families with incomes under $5,000 a year, for a poverty limitation on college attendance is intolerable. This broad program, we may be sure, would receive the benign approval of Horace Greeley, Ezra Cornell, and Andrew D. White, who were struggling a century ago to bring to realization their dream of higher education for the whole people; the dream first given national character and strong impetus by the Morrill Land-Grant Act.

An impressive feature of the New York report is its insistence that slackness and inefficiency be banished from our whole educational system. The minimum level of attainment in high schools, colleges, and universities should be raised; students should be encouraged to study all year round, on a forty-eight-week basis, and take the bachelor's degree in three years, the master's in four; classrooms, libraries, and laboratories should be in full use day and evening, including Saturdays; and the opportunity for college-level education should be expanded in a great diversity of fields by establishment of a state-wide network of educational television. This last, of course, will require superior teachers, effective organization of courses, and careful supplementary work in discussion sections, workshops, and laboratory experiments. Already we begin to start our pupils in school, after the English fashion, at age five instead of six, to lengthen our school terms, and to arrange for advanced placement of brilliant students in college. The New York committee, calling for vast new state expenditures, insists that the money be used with a minimum of waste and a maximum of profit.

Efficiency is not attained without hard labor — and courage. A state-wide system of coordinated universities and colleges offers dangers as well as advantages; and while its adoption in the states of largest area and population seems inescapable, it should be created without surrender to special pressures. As President Truman's committee on education beyond high school declared, new programs should not be provided at the expense of the normal evolution of the educational resources we now have. The states which have mountain ranges rising find that local appetites for another spur of the range can be troublesome. California with her sixteen state colleges hears a clamor from twenty more counties: "We are neglected; let us have a college too; it will cost less than to expand the State university." What they really mean is often, "We want the college payroll, the convenience and the prestige." Heads of the California system have to labor amain to persuade these communities that more colleges would be unwise. Former President James L. Morrill of Minnesota writes that when a commission representing both the public and endowed institutions of the state reported in favor of six new junior colleges, at once a clamor arose for five times that number. But the tendency is right, and just solutions, with courage, can be evolved.

At the beginning we said that the principal idea, among many, that entered into the founding of the land-grant colleges was the democratic idea; the principle that the rising generation in America should have free opportunity, including free access to all major occupations on a professional level, and thus be able to maintain an open and mobile society. The Morrill Act embodied this principle. The response of the people to it was gradual, but by 1910 it had become so general and enthusiastic that the initial problems of survival gave way to problems of exuberant growth. A half-century later, in 1961, the public universities have reached a new plane of development. They are now the most important sector of higher education in the country — nay, on the globe. The central task, in at least the richer and better-developed states, is that of continued and even gigantic growth with a proper separation of talents; of giving all an opportunity, but fixing proper channels and gradations of opportunity.

The fundamental question remains just what it was at the outset: what can the state universities and land-grant institutions, in their newest phase, do for democracy? How can they equip the rising generation for the free access of talent to appropriate callings and thus maintain an open society?

They realize more than ever that they must strive through research and experimentation, and through bold innovation in the arts, to give new benefits to the whole people and lend touches of distinction to their lives. They realize that they must make good in modern ways, with the best instruments of the mass media, the boast they first made two generations ago, that the limits of the state are the limits of the campus. Above all, they know that they must provide a future for the almost overwhelming masses of young people whom the high schools throw, or will soon throw, on their doorsteps, and do it with proper discrimination and selectivity. Happily, they front the new century with more zeal, more conscientiousness, and far more talent than they ever commanded before. They will answer the challenge, and answering it, give still fuller justification to the truly epochal work that Justin S. Morrill began, and that White, Gilman, Angell, Van Hise, James, and so many more gallantly carried on.

* * *

BIBLIOGRAPHICAL NOTE

An ample bibliographical apparatus on the land-grant institutions, and to a great extent the state universities, whether land-grant or not, is contained in two standard volumes, Earle D. Ross, *Democracy's College; The Land-Grant Movement in the Formative Stage* (Ames: Iowa State College Press, 1942), 231-254; and Edward Danforth Eddy, Jr., *Colleges for Our Land and Time: The Land-Grant Idea in American Education* (New York: Harper and Brothers, 1956), 302-317.

The titles listed therein are supplemented by the catalogues or course announcements of the various institutions; by the annual reports of the presidents, which vary in length from less than fifty pages for the heads of the Universities of Wisconsin or Texas to nearly five hundred pages for the University of Michigan; and by a great variety of special bulletins and brochures, often attractively illustrated. The American Association of Land-Grant Colleges and State

Universities, to use the present name of the body, published its first convention proceedings in 1885 and 1887, and continues them in regular volumes.

Among the more valuable of recent publications on the ideals, practical aims, and problems of the state universities and land-grant colleges may be mentioned David D. Henry's *What Priority for Education? The American People Must Soon Decide* (1961), James Lewis Morrill's *The Ongoing State University* (1960), and Logan Wilson's (ed.) *The State University* (1959). They are the work respectively of the president of the University of Illinois, the former president of the University of Minnesota, and the former president of the University of Texas.

(✧)

Appendix

THE FOLLOWING list supplied by the Institute for International Education includes accredited land-grant colleges and state universities which are members of the American Association of Land-Grant Colleges and State Universities and of the State Universities Association. Information on type of control, level of studies offered, composition of student body, and total enrollment is taken from the *Education Directory, 1959-1960, Part 3, Higher Education,* published by the U.S. Department of Health, Education, and Welfare.

The abbreviations used are as follows:

l.g.: land-grant institution

pub.: controlled by municipal, county, state, territorial, district, or federal government

priv.: controlled by private corporation, independent of church

coed.: student body composed of men and women

men: student body composed of men

wo.: student body composed of women

U.: undergraduate only

G.: also has graduate division

The figure given for each institution indicates total enrollment in 1959-60; but in many instances

[141]

these include extension course students, and are to be taken with reserve.

ALABAMA

Alabama Agricultural and Mechanical College, Normal: l.g., pub., coed., U., 1,077.

Auburn University, Auburn: l.g., pub., coed., G., 8,517.

University of Alabama, University: pub., coed., G., 13,013.

ALASKA

University of Alaska, College: l.g., pub., coed., G., 1,977.

ARIZONA

Arizona State University, Tempe: pub., coed., G., 10,561.

University of Arizona, Tucson: l.g., pub., coed., G., 11,393.

ARKANSAS

Agricultural, Mechanical and Normal College, Pine Bluff: l.g., pub., coed., U., 1,353.

University of Arkansas, Fayetteville: l.g., pub., coed., G., 6,155.

CALIFORNIA

University of California, campuses at Berkeley, Davis, La Jolla, Los Angeles, Riverside, Santa Barbara, San Francisco, etc.: l.g., pub., coed., G., 43,478.

COLORADO

Colorado State University, Fort Collins: l.g., pub., coed., G., 5,593.

University of Colorado, Boulder: pub., coed., G., 18,800.

CONNECTICUT

University of Connecticut, Storrs: l.g., pub., coed., G., 10,492.

DELAWARE

Delaware State College, Dover: l.g., pub., coed., U., 294.

University of Delaware, Newark: l.g., pub., coed., G., 5,777.

FLORIDA

Florida Agricultural and Mechanical University, Tallahassee: l.g., pub., coed., G., 3,038.

Florida State University, Tallahassee: pub., coed., G., 9,569.

University of Florida, Gainesville: l.g., pub., coed., G., 15,678.

GEORGIA

Fort Valley State College, Fort Valley: l.g., pub., coed., G., 795.

Georgia Institute of Technology, Atlanta: pub., coed., G., 6,493.

University of Georgia, Athens: l.g., pub., coed., G., 10,716.

HAWAII

University of Hawaii, Honolulu: l.g., pub., coed., G., 7,906.

IDAHO

University of Idaho, Moscow: l.g., pub., coed., G., 4,131.

ILLINOIS

University of Illinois, Urbana: l.g., pub., coed., G., 27,089.

INDIANA

Indiana University, Bloomington: pub., coed., G., 23,531.

Purdue University, Lafayette: l.g., pub., coed., G., 15,763.

IOWA

Iowa State University of Science and Technology, Ames: l.g., pub., coed., G., 9,503.

State University of Iowa, Iowa City: pub., coed., G., 10,516.

KANSAS

Kansas State University of Agriculture and Applied Science, Manhattan: l.g., pub., coed., G., 8,180.

University of Kansas, Lawrence: pub., coed., G., 9,241.

KENTUCKY

Kentucky State College, Frankfort: l.g., pub., coed., U., 581.

University of Kentucky, Lexington: l.g., pub., coed., G., 9,612.

LOUISIANA

Louisiana State University and Agricultural and Mechanical College, Baton Rouge: l.g., pub., coed., G., 11,948.

Southern University and Agricultural and Mechanical College, Baton Rouge: l.g., pub., coed., G., 4,889.

MAINE

University of Maine, Orono: l.g., pub., coed., G., 5,697.

MARYLAND

University of Maryland, College Park: l.g., pub., coed., G., 18,141.

Maryland State College, Princess Anne: l.g., pub., coed., U., 427.

MASSACHUSETTS

Massachusetts Institute of Technology, Cambridge: l.g., priv., coed., G., 6,233.

University of Massachusetts, Amherst: l.g., pub., coed., G., 5,030.

MICHIGAN

Michigan State University of Agriculture and Applied Science, East Lansing: l.g., pub., coed., G., 20,549.

University of Michigan, Ann Arbor: pub., coed., G., 26,581.

Wayne State University, Detroit: pub., coed., G., 20,208.

MINNESOTA

University of Minnesota, Minneapolis: l.g., pub., coed., G., 36,288.

MISSISSIPPI

Alcorn Agricultural and Mechanical College, Lorman: l.g., pub., coed., U., 775.

Mississippi State University, State College: l.g., pub., coed., G., 4,884.

University of Mississippi, University: pub., coed., G., 4,149.

MISSOURI

Lincoln University, Jefferson City: l.g., pub., coed., G., 1,354.

University of Missouri, Columbia: l.g., pub., coed., G., 14,422.

MONTANA

Montana State College, Bozeman: l.g., pub., coed., G., 3,835.

Montana State University, Missoula: pub., coed., G., 3,337.

NEBRASKA

University of Nebraska, Lincoln: l.g., pub., coed., G., 11,652.

NEVADA

University of Nevada, Reno: l.g., pub., coed., G., 3,354.

NEW HAMPSHIRE

University of New Hampshire, Durham: l.g., pub., coed., G., 4,287.

NEW JERSEY

Rutgers University, The State University of New Jersey, New Brunswick: l.g., pub., men, wo., G., 14,779.

NEW MEXICO

New Mexico State University of Agriculture, University Park: l.g., pub., coed., G., 3,605.

University of New Mexico, Albuquerque: pub., coed., G., 6,994.

NEW YORK

Cornell University, Ithaca: l.g., pub. and priv., coed., G., 11,184.

State University of New York, Albany: l.g., pub., coed., G., 32,196.

NORTH CAROLINA

Agricultural and Technical College of North Carolina, Greensboro: l.g., pub., coed., G., 2,633.

North Carolina State College of Agriculture and Engineering, Raleigh: l.g., pub., coed., G., 6,380.

University of North Carolina, Chapel Hill: l.g., pub., coed., G., 7,513.

NORTH DAKOTA

North Dakota Agricultural College, Fargo: l.g., pub., coed., G., 3,250.

University of North Dakota, Grand Forks: pub., coed., G., 4,089.

OHIO

Miami University, Oxford: pub., coed., G., 8,654.

Ohio State University, Columbus: l.g., pub., coed., G., 23,164.

Ohio University, Athens: pub., coed., G., 10,004.

OKLAHOMA

Langston University, Langston: l.g., pub., coed., U., 544.

Oklahoma State University of Agriculture and Applied Science, Stillwater: l.g., pub., coed., G., 10,544.

University of Oklahoma, Norman: pub., coed., G., 12,221.

OREGON

Oregon State College, Corvallis: l.g., pub., coed., G., 7,979.

University of Oregon, Eugene: pub., coed., G., 7,078.

PENNSYLVANIA

Pennsylvania State University, University Park: l.g., pub., coed., G., 16,543.

PUERTO RICO

University of Puerto Rico, Rio Piedras: l.g., pub., coed., G., 17,599.

RHODE ISLAND

University of Rhode Island, Kingston: l.g., pub., coed., G., 4,494.

SOUTH CAROLINA

Clemson Agricultural College, Clemson: l.g., pub., coed., G., 3,793.

South Carolina State College, Orangeburg: l.g., pub., coed., G., 1,860.

University of South Carolina, Columbia: pub., coed., G., 7,469.

SOUTH DAKOTA

South Dakota State College of Agriculture and Mechanic Arts, Brookings: l.g., pub., coed., G., 3,822.

State University of South Dakota, Vermillion: pub., coed., G., 2,673.

TENNESSEE

Tennessee Agricultural and Industrial State University, Nashville: l.g., pub., coed., G., 2,981.

University of Tennessee, Knoxville: l.g., pub., coed., G., 15,560.

TEXAS

Agricultural and Mechanical College of Texas, College Station: l.g., pub., men, G., 7,073.

Prairie View Agricultural and Mechanical College, Prairie View: l.g., pub., coed., G., 2,664.

University of Texas, Austin: pub., coed., G., 19,508.

UTAH

University of Utah, Salt Lake City: pub., coed., G., 10,711.

Utah State University of Agriculture and Applied Science, Logan: l.g., pub., coed., G., 5,672.

VERMONT

University of Vermont and State Agricultural College, Burlington: l.g., pub., coed., G., 3,220.

VIRGINIA

University of Virginia, Charlottesville: pub., men, wo., G., 13,831.

Virginia Polytechnic Institute, Blacksburg: l.g., pub., coed., G., 6,274.

Virginia State College, Petersburg: l.g., pub., coed., G., 2,633.

WASHINGTON

University of Washington, Seattle: pub., coed., G., 20,411.

Washington State University, Pullman: l.g., pub., coed., G., 6,786.

WEST VIRGINIA

West Virginia University, Morgantown: l.g., pub., coed., G., 7,093.

WISCONSIN

University of Wisconsin, Madison: l.g., pub., coed., G., 26,678.

WYOMING

University of Wyoming, Laramie: l.g., pub., coed., G., 4,206.

(✠)

Index

Accreditation: stimulates spirit of community pride, 47; system of, for secondary schools, 92

Adams, Charles Kendall, 90

Adams, John Quincy: protagonist of scientific studies, 8

Addams, Jane: describes earnestness among Rockford College students, 74

Administrators, university: function of, in early period, 94; a new type of, emerges, 113; vital requirement for proper function of universities, 118-120

Admissions: standards for, remain deplorable, 117; improvement of standards of, 129-131; effective screening of, 134-135. *See also* Registration, land-grant institutions; Enrollment

Aeschuylus, 90

Agassiz, Alexander: accepts professorship at Harvard, 9; teaches at Cornell, 48; mentioned, 51, 103

Agricultural chemistry: study of, begun at Yale, 10

Agricultural colleges: Michigan, Maryland, and Pennsylvania have first, 15

Agriculture: Porter offers ante bellum course in, 10; to hold equal position with liberal arts, 11-12; colleges of, promoted by public, 13; establishment of, as field of study, 13-14; leaders of, oppose classical training, 48; attacks literary tradition and land-grant movement, 53-54; struggle to establish courses in, 55-62; development of, as course of study, 60-65; study of, aided by Hatch Act, 68n; fully established as science, 86-87; diversification of, in many

California, 1872, 65; says scholars, writers, and teachers important element, 103; mentioned, 118, 139

Godkin, E. L., 52

Goethe, Johann Wolfgang von, 90

Goldsmith, Oliver, 130

Goodrich, S. G.: and *Recollections of a Lifetime,* 14n; and *Peter Parley's Book,* 20

Graduate schools: establishment of, 100-101; growth and importance of, 122-123; importance of research in, 123-124; mentioned, 112, 114

Graham, Mentor, 20

Grange: leaders of, threaten university, 56

Grangerism, 27

Grant, Ulysses S.: sordid administration of, 22; errors of, mar decade, 26

Greeley, Horace: popularly leads revolt against classics, 5; presses for agricultural skills, 11; applies democratic principle to education, 16; and requirement of democracy for education, 17n; asserts agriculture a noble science, 55; preferred unschooled journalists, 128; mentioned, 98, 136

Greenback-Labor crusade, 27

Greene, Evart B.: teaches history, 103

Gregory, John Milton: receives keys for University of Illinois, 1868, 24; and task of transforming democracy, 25; receives salary of $4,000 a year, 32; administration of, described, 36; heads Illinois with inadequate clerical help, 49; holds ground in conflict, 57; declares agriculture not a science, 57; mentioned, 24n, 62, 65, 86

Grimm, brothers: aid University of Berlin, 3

Griswold, A. Whitney, 131

Growth, university: four essential elements of, 92-93; controlled by time-size-resources equation, 117-118

Guizot, François: history book of, broadening influence, 4; and *History of Civilization in Europe,* 4n; mentioned, 5

Hadley, Arthur Twining: says Western universities provincial, 75

Hall, Baynard R.: example of land-grant university pioneer, 41

Hard, William, 98

Harper, William Rainey: encourages Van Hise, 97; mentioned, 93, 119

Harris, William Torrey: defines American idea of secondary education, 91